THE SO-CALLED OCCULT

THE SO-CALLED OCCULT

On the Psychology and Pathology
of So-Called Occult Phenomena

C.G. Jung

JABBERWOKE
San Francisco

TheSoCalledOccult.com

Contents

THE SO-CALLED OCCULT

I

ON THE PSYCHOLOGY AND PATHOLOGY OF SO-CALLED OCCULT PHENOMENA

IN THAT WIDE field of psychopathic deficiency where Science has demarcated the diseases of epilepsy, hysteria and neurasthenia, we meet scattered observations concerning certain rare states of consciousness as to whose meaning authors are not yet agreed. These observations spring up sporadically in the literature on narcolepsy, lethargy, periodic amnesia, double consciousness, somnambulism, *automatisme ambulatoire*, pathological dreamy states, pathological lying, etc.

These states are sometimes attributed to epilepsy, sometimes to hysteria, sometimes to exhaustion of the nervous system, or neurasthenia, sometimes they are allowed all the dignity of a disease *sui generis*. Patients occasionally work through a whole graduated scale of diagnoses, from epilepsy, through hysteria, up to simulation. In practice, on the one hand, these conditions can only be separated with great difficulty from the so-called neuroses, sometimes even are indistinguishable from them; on the other, certain features in the region of pathological deficiency present more than a mere analogical relationship not only with phenomena of normal psychology, but also with the psychology of the supernormal, of genius. Various as are the individual phenomena in this region, there is certainly no case that cannot be connected by some intermediate example with the other typical cases. This relationship in the pictures presented by hysteria and epilepsy is very close. Recently the view has even been maintained that there is no clean-cut frontier between epilepsy and hysteria, and that a difference is only to be noted in extreme cases. Steffens says, for example, "We are forced to the conclusion that in essence hysteria and epilepsy are not fundamentally different, that the cause of the disease is the same, but is manifest in a diverse form, in different intensity and permanence."[°]

The demarcation of hysteria and certain borderline cases of epilepsy from congenital and acquired psychopathic mental deficiency likewise presents the greatest difficulties. The symptoms of one or other disease everywhere invade the neighbouring realm, so violence is done to the facts when they are split off and considered as belonging to one or other realm. The demarcation of psychopathic mental deficiency from the normal is an absolutely impossible task, the difference is everywhere

---

° *Arch. f. Psych.*, XXXIII. p. 928.

only "more or less." The classification in the region of mental deficiency itself is confronted by the same difficulty. At best, certain classes can be separated off which crystallise round some well-marked nucleus through having peculiarly typical features. Turning away from the two large groups of intellectual and emotional deficiency, there remain those deficiencies coloured pre-eminently by hysteria or epilepsy (epileptoid) or neurasthenia, which are not notably deficiency of the intellect or of feeling. It is essentially in this region, insusceptible of any absolute classification, that the above-named conditions play their part. As is well known, they can appear as part manifestations of a typical epilepsy or hysteria, or can exist separately in the realm of psychopathic mental deficiency, where their qualifications of epileptic or hysterical are often due to the non-essential accessory features. It is thus the rule to place somnambulism among hysterical diseases, because it is occasionally a phenomenon of severe hysteria, or because mild so-called hysterical symptoms may accompany it. As one of the manifestations of a severe hysteria, somnambulism is not an unknown phenomenon, but as a pathological entity, as a disease *sui generis*, it must be somewhat rare, to judge by its infrequency in German literature on the subject. So-called spontaneous somnambulism, resting upon a foundation of hysterically-tinged psychopathic deficiency, is not a very common occurrence and it is worth while to devote closer study to these cases, for they occasionally present a mass of interesting particulars.

In the region of psychopathic deficiency with hysterical colouring, we encounter numerous phenomena which show, as in this case, symptoms of diverse defined diseases, which cannot be attributed with certainty to any one of them. These phenomena are partially recognised to be independent; for instance, pathological lying, pathological reveries, etc. Many of these states, however, still await thorough scientific investigation; at present they belong more or less to the domain of scientific gossip. Persons with habitual hallucinations, and also the inspired, exhibit these states; they draw the attention of the crowd to themselves, now as poet or artist, now as saviour, prophet or founder of a new sect.

The genesis of the peculiar frame of mind of these persons is for the most part lost in obscurity, for it is only very rarely that one of these remarkable personalities can be subjected to exact observation. In view of the often great historical importance of these persons, it is much to be wished that we had some scientific material which would enable us to gain a closer insight into the psychological development of their peculiarities. Apart from the now practically useless productions of the pneumatological school at the beginning of the nineteenth century, German scientific literature is very poor in this respect; indeed, there seems to be real aversion from investigation in this field. For the facts so far gathered we are indebted almost exclusively to the labours of French and English workers. It seems at least desirable that our literature should be enlarged in this respect. These considerations have induced me to publish some observations which will perhaps help to further our knowledge concerning the relationship of hysterical twilight-states and enlarge the problems of normal psychology.

Helene Preiswerk

II

CASE OF SONAMBULISM IN A
GIRL WITH NEUROPATHIC
INHERITANCE

THE FOLLOWING CASE was under my observation in the years 1899 and 1900. As I was
not in medical attendance upon Miss S. W.,°
a physical examination for hysterical stigmata
unfortunately could not be made. I kept a
complete diary of the séances, which I filled
up after each sitting. The following report is a
condensed account from these notes. Out of
regard for Miss S. W. and her family a few
unimportant dates have been altered and a
few details omitted from the story, which for
the most part is composed of very intimate
matters.

Miss S. W., 15½ years old. Reformed
Church. The paternal grandfather was highly
intelligent, a clergyman with frequent waking
hallucinations (generally visions, often whole
dramatic scenes with dialogues, etc.). A
brother of the grandfather was an imbecile eccentric, who also saw visions. A sister of the

---

° [Ed. – Real name Helene Preiswerk (1881-1911),
Carl Jung's maternal cousin.]

grandfather, a peculiar, odd character. The paternal grandmother after some fever in her 20th year (typhoid?) had a trance which lasted three days, from which she did not awake until the crown of her head had been burned by a red-hot iron. During states of excitement later on she had fainting fits which were nearly always followed by a brief somnambulism during which she uttered prophesies. Her father was likewise a peculiar, original personality with bizarre ideas. All three had waking hallucinations (second-sight, forebodings, etc.). A third brother was also eccentric and odd, talented but one-sided. The mother has an inherited mental defect often bordering on psychosis. The sister is a hysteric and visionary and a second sister suffers from "nervous heart attacks." Miss S. W. is slenderly built, skull somewhat rachitic, without pronounced hydrocephalus, face rather pale, eyes dark with a peculiar penetrating look. She has had no serious illnesses. At school she passed for average, showed little interest, was inattentive. As a rule her behaviour was rather reserved, sometimes giving place, however, to exuberant joy and exaltation. Of average intelligence, without special gifts, neither musical nor fond of books, her preference is for handwork—and day dreaming. She was often absent-minded, misread in a peculiar way when reading aloud, instead of the word *ziege* (goat), for instance, said *gais*, instead of *treppe* (stair), *stege*; this occurred so often that her brothers and sisters laughed at her. There were no other abnormalities; there were no serious hysterical manifestations. Her family were artisans and business people with very limited interests. Books of mystical content were never permitted in the family. Her education was faulty; there were numerous brothers and sisters and thus the education was given indiscriminately, and in addition the children had to suffer a great deal from the inconsequent and vulgar, indeed sometimes rough, treatment of their mother. The father, a very busy business man, could not pay much attention to his children, and died when S. W. was not yet grown up. Under these uncomfortable conditions it is no wonder that S. W. felt herself shut in and unhappy. She was often afraid to go home, and preferred to be anywhere rather than there. She was left a great deal with playmates and grew up in this way without much polish. The level of her education is relatively low and her interests correspondingly limited. Her knowledge of literature is also very limited. She knows the common school songs by heart, songs of Schiller and Goethe and a few other poets, as well as fragments from a song book and the psalms. Newspaper stories represent her highest level in prose. Up to the time of her somnambulism she had never read any books of a serious nature. At home and from friends she heard about table-turning and began to take an interest in it. She asked to be allowed to take part in such experiments, and her desire was soon gratified. In July 1899, she took part a few times in table-turnings with some friends and her brothers and sisters, but in joke. It was then discovered that she was an excellent "medium." Some communications of a serious nature arrived which were received with general astonishment. Their pastoral tone was surprising. The spirit said he was the grandfather of the medium. As I was acquainted with the family I was able to take part in these experiments. At the beginning of August, 1899, the first attacks of somnambulism took place in my presence. They took the following course: S. W. became very pale, slowly sank to the ground, or into a chair, shut her eyes, became cataleptic, drew several deep breaths, and began to speak. In this stage she was generally quite relaxed; the reflexes of the lids remained, as did also tactile sensation. She was sensitive to unexpected noises and full of fear, especially in the initial stage.

She did not react when called by name. In somnambulic dialogues she copied in a remarkably clever way her dead relations and acquaintances, with all their peculiarities, so that she made a lasting impression upon unprejudiced persons. She also so closely imitated persons whom she only knew from descriptions that no one could deny her at least considerable talent as an actress. Gradually gestures were added to the simple speech, which finally led to *"attitudes passionelles"* and complete dramatic scenes. She took up postures of prayer and rapture, with staring eyes, and spoke with impassionate and glowing rhetoric. She then made use exclusively of a literary German which she spoke with an ease and assurance quite contrary to her usual uncertain and embarrassed manner in the waking state. Her movements were free and of a noble grace, depicting most beautifully her varying emotions. Her attitude during these states was always changing and diverse in the different attacks. Now she would lie for ten minutes to two hours on the sofa or the ground, motionless, with closed eyes; now she assumed a half-sitting posture and spoke with changed tone and speech; now she would stand up, going through every possible pantomimic gesture. Her speech was equally diversified and without rule. Now she spoke in the first person, but never for long, generally to prophesy her next attack; now she spoke of herself (and this was the most usual) in the third person. She then acted as some other person, either some dead acquaintance or some chance person, whose part she consistently carried out according to the characteristics she herself conceived. At the end of the ecstasy there usually followed a cataleptic state with *flexibilitas cerea*, which gradually passed over into the waking state. The waxy anæmic pallor which was an almost constant feature of the attacks made one really anxious; it sometimes occurred at the beginning of the attack, but often in the second half only. The pulse was then small but regular and of normal frequency; the breathing gentle, shallow, or almost imperceptible. As already stated, S. W. often predicted her attacks beforehand; just before the attacks she had strange sensations, became excited, rather anxious, and occasionally expressed thoughts of death: "she will probably die in one of these attacks; "during the attack her soul only hangs to her body by a thread, so that often the body could scarcely go on living." Once after the cataleptic attack tachypnœa lasting two minutes was observed, with a respiration rate of 100 per minute. At first the attacks occurred spontaneously, afterwards S. W. could provoke them by sitting in a dark corner and covering her face with her hands. Frequently the experiment did not succeed. She had so-called "good" and "bad" days. The question of amnesia after the attacks is unfortunately very obscure. This much is certain, that after each attack she was quite accurately orientated as to what she had gone through "during the rapture." It is, however, uncertain how much she remembered of the conversations in which she served as medium, and of changes in her surroundings during the attack. It often seemed that she did havex a fleeting recollection, for directly after waking she would ask: "Who was here? Wasn't X or Y here? What did he say?" She also showed that she was superficially aware of the content of the conversations. She thus often remarked that the spirits had communicated to her before waking what they had said. But frequently this was not the case. If, at her request, the contents of the trance speeches were repeated to her she was often annoyed about them. She was then often sad and depressed for hours together, especially when any unpleasant indiscretions had occurred. She would then rail against the spirits and assert that next time she would beg her guides to keep such spirits far away. Her indignation was not feigned, for in the waking state she could but poorly control herself and her emotions, so that every mood was at once mirrored in her face. At times she seemed only slightly or not at all aware of the external proceedings during the attack. She seldom noticed when any one left the room or came in. Once she forbade me to enter the room when she was awaiting special communications which she wished to keep secret from me.

Nevertheless I went in, and sat down with the three other sitters and listened to everything. Her eyes were open and she spoke to those present without noticing me. She only noticed me when I began to speak, which gave rise to a storm of indignation. She remembered better, but still apparently only in indefinite outlines, the remarks of those taking part which referred to the trance speeches or directly to herself. I could never discover any definite rapport in this connection.

In addition to these great attacks which seemed to follow a certain law in their course, S. W. produced a great number of other automatisms. Premonitions, forebodings, unaccountable moods and rapidly changing fancies were all in the day's work. I never observed simple states of sleep. On the other hand, I soon noticed that in the middle of a lively conversation S. W. became quite confused and spoke without meaning in a peculiar monotonous way, and looked in front of her dreamily with half-closed eyes. These lapses usually lasted but a few minutes. Then she would suddenly proceed: "Yes, what did you say?" At first she would not give any particulars about these lapses, she would reply off-hand that she was a little giddy, had a headache, and so on. Later she simply said: "they were there again," meaning her spirits. She was subjected to the lapses much against her will; she often tried to defend herself: "I do not want to, not now, come some other time; you seem to think I only exist for you." She had these lapses in the streets, in business, in fact anywhere. If this happened to her in the street, she leaned against a house and waited till the attack was over. During these attacks, whose intensity was most variable, she had visions; frequently also, especially during the attacks where she turned extremely pale, she "wandered"; or as she expressed it, lost her body, and got away to distant places whither her spirits led her. Distant journeys during ecstasy strained her exceedingly; she was often exhausted for hours after, and many times complained that the spirits had again deprived her of much power, such overstrain was now too much for her; the spirits must get another medium, etc. Once she was hysterically blind for half an hour after one of these ecstasies. Her gait was hesitating, feeling her way; she had to be led; she did not see the candle which was on the table. The pupils reacted. Visions occurred in great numbers without proper "lapses" (designating by this word only the higher grade of distraction of attention). At first the visions only occurred at the beginning of the sleep. Once after S. W. had gone to bed the room became lighted up, and out of the general foggy light there appeared white glittering figures. They were throughout concealed in white veil-like robes, the women had a head-covering like a turban, and a girdle. Afterwards (according to the statements of S. W.), "the spirits were already there" when she went to bed. Finally she also saw the figures in bright daylight, though still somewhat blurred and only for a short time, provided there were no proper lapses, in which case the figures became solid enough to take hold of. But S. W. always preferred darkness. According to her account the content of the vision was for the most part of a pleasant kind. Gazing at the beautiful figures she received a feeling of delicious blessedness. More rarely there were terrible visions of a dæmonic nature. These were entirely confined to the night or to dark rooms. Occasionally S. W. saw black figures in the neighbouring streets or in her room; once out in the dark courtyard she saw a terrible copper-red face which suddenly stared at her and frightened her. I could not learn anything satisfactory about the first occurrence of the vision. She states that once at night, in her fifth or sixth year, she saw her "guide," her grandfather (whom she had never known). I could not get any objective confirmation from her relatives of this early vision. Nothing of the kind is said to have happened until her first séance. With the exception of the hypnagogic brightness and the flashes, there were no rudimentary hallucinations, but from the beginning they were of a systematic nature, involving all the sense-organs equally. So far as concerns the intellectual reaction to these phenomena it is remarkable with what curious sincerity she regarded her dreams. Her entire somnambulic development, the innumerable puzzling events, seemed to her quite natural. She looked at her whole past in this light. Every striking event of earlier years stood to her in necessary and clear relationship to her present condition. She was happy in the consciousness of having found her real life-task. Naturally she was unswervingly convinced of the reality of her visions. I often tried to present her with some sceptical explanation, but she invariably turned this aside; in her usual condition she did not clearly grasp a reasoned explanation, and in the semi-somnambulic state she regarded it as senseless in view of the facts staring her in the face. She once said: "I do not know if what the spirits say and teach me is true, neither do I know if they are those by whose names they call themselves, but that my spirits exist there is no question. I see them before me, I can touch them, I speak to them about everything I wish, as naturally as I'm now talking to you. They must be real." She absolutely would not listen to the idea that the manifestations were a kind of illness. Doubts about her health or about the reality of her dream would distress her deeply; she felt so hurt by my remarks that when I was present she became reserved, and for a long time refused to experiment if I was there; hence I took care not to express my doubts and thoughts aloud. From her immediate relatives and acquaintances she received undivided allegiance and admiration—they asked her advice about all kinds of things. In time she obtained such an influence upon her followers that three of her brothers and sisters likewise began to have hallucinations of a similar kind. Their hallucinations generally began as night-dreams of a very vivid and dramatic kind; these gradually extended into the waking time, partly hypnagogic, partly hypnopompic. A married sister had extraordinary vivid dreams which developed from night to night, and these appeared in the waking consciousness; at first as obscure illusions, next as real hallucinations, but they never reached the plastic clearness of S. W.'s visions. For instance, she once saw in a dream a black dæmonic figure at her bedside in animated conversation with a white, beautiful figure, which tried to restrain the black one; nevertheless the black one seized her and tried to choke her, then she awoke. Bending over her she then saw a black shadow with a human contour, and near by a white cloudy figure. The vision only disappeared when she lighted a candle. Similar visions were repeated dozens of times. The visions of the other two sisters were of a similar kind, but less intense.

This particular type of attack with the complete visions and ideas had developed in the course of less than a month, but never afterwards exceeded these limits. What was later added to these was but the extension of all those thoughts and cycles of visions which to a certain extent were already indicated quite at the beginning. As well as the "great" attacks and the lesser ones, there must also be noted a third kind of state comparable to "lapse" states. These are the *semi-somnambulic states*. They appeared at the beginning or at the end of the "great" attacks, but also appeared without any connection with them. They developed gradually in the course of the first month. It is not possible to give a more precise account of the time of their appearance. In this state a fixed gaze, brilliant eyes, and a certain dignity and stateliness of movement are noticeable. In this phase S. W. is herself, her own somnambulic ego.

She is fully orientated to the external world, but seems to stand with one foot, as it were, in her dream-world. She sees and hears her spirits, sees how they walk about in the room among those who form the circle, and stand first by one person, then by another. She is in possession of a clear remembrance of her visions, her journeys and the instructions she receives. She speaks quietly, clearly and firmly and is always in a serious, almost religious frame of mind. Her bearing indicates a deeply religious mood, free from all pietistic flavour, her speech is singularly uninfluenced by her guide's jargon compounded of Bible and tract. Her solemn behaviour has a suffering, rather pitiful aspect. She is painfully conscious of the great differences between her ideal world at night and the rough reality of the day. This state stands in sharp contrast to her waking existence; there is here no trace of that unstable and inharmonious creature, that extravagant nervous temperament which is so characteristic for the rest of her relationships. Speaking with her, you get the impression of speaking with a much older person who has attained through numerous experiences to a sure harmonious footing. In this state she produced her best results, whilst her romances correspond more closely to the conditions of her waking interests. The semi-somnambulism usually appears spontaneously, mostly during the table experiments, which sometimes announced by this means that S. W. was beginning to know beforehand every automatic communication from the table. She then usually stopped the table-turning and after a short time passed more or less suddenly into an ecstatic state. S. W. showed herself to be very sensitive. She could divine and reply to simple questions thought of by a member of the circle who was not a "medium," if only the latter would lay a hand on the table or on her hand. Genuine thought-transference without direct or indirect contact could never be achieved. In juxtaposition with the obvious development of her whole personality the continued existence of her earlier ordinary character was all the more startling. She imparted with unconcealed pleasure all the little childish experiences, the flirtations and love-secrets, all the rudeness and lack of education of her parents and contemporaries. To every one who did not know her secret she was a girl of fifteen and a half, in no respect unlike a thousand other such girls. So much the greater was people's astonishment when they got to know her in her other aspect. Her near relatives could not at first grasp this change: to some extent they never altogether understood it, so there was often bitter strife in the family, some of them taking sides for and others against S. W., either with enthusiastic over-valuation or with contemptuous censure of "superstition." Thus did S. W., during the time I watched her closely, lead a curious, contradictory life, a real "double life" with two personalities existing side by side or closely following upon one another and contending for the mastery. I now give some of the most interesting details of the sittings in chronological order.

First and second sittings, August, 1899. S. W. at once undertook to lead the "communications." The "psychograph," for which an upturned glass tumbler was used, on which two fingers of the right hand were laid, moved quick as lightning from letter to letter. (Slips of paper, marked with letter and numbers, had been arranged in a circle round the glass.) It was communicated that the "medium's" grandfather was present and would speak to us. There then followed many communications in quick sequence, of a most religious, edifying nature, in part in properly made words, partly in words with the letters transposed, and partly in a series of reversed letters. The last words and sentences were produced so quickly that it was not possible to follow without first inverting the letters. The communications were once interrupted in abrupt fashion by a new communication, which announced the presence of the writer's grandfather. On this occasion the jesting observation was made: "Evidently the two 'spirits' get on very badly together." During this attempt darkness came on. Suddenly S. W. became very disturbed, sprang up in terror, fell on her knees and cried "There, there, do you not see that light, that star there?" and pointed to a dark corner of the room. She became more and more disturbed, and called for a light in terror. She was pale, wept, "it was all so strange, she did not know in the least what was the matter with her." When a candle was brought she became calm again. The experiments were now stopped.

At the next sitting, which took place in the evening, two days later, similar communications from S. W.'s grandfather were obtained. When darkness fell S. W. suddenly leaned back on the sofa, grew pale, almost shut her eyes, and lay there motionless. The eyeballs were turned upwards, the lid-reflex was present as well as tactile sensation. The breathing was gentle, almost imperceptible. The pulse small and weak. This attack lasted about half an hour, when S. W. suddenly sighed and got up. The extreme pallor, which had lasted throughout the whole attack, now gave place to her usual pale pink colour. She was somewhat confused and distraught, indicated that she had seen all sorts of things, but would tell nothing. Only after urgent questioning would she relate that in an extraordinary waking condition she had seen her grandfather arm-in-arm with the writer's grandfather. The two had gone rapidly by in an open carriage, side by side.

III. In the third séance, which took place some days later, there was a similar attack of more than half an hour's duration. S. W.

afterwards told of many white, transfigured forms who each gave her a flower of special symbolic significance. Most of them were dead relatives. Concerning the exact content of their talk she maintained an obstinate silence.

IV. After S. W. had entered into the somnambulic state she began to make curious movements with her lips, and made swallowing gurgling noises. Then she whispered very softly and unintelligibly. When this had lasted some minutes she suddenly began to speak in an altered deep voice. She spoke of herself in the third person. "She is not here, she has gone away." There followed several communications of a religious kind. From the content and the way of speaking it was easy to conclude that she was imitating her grandfather, who had been a clergyman. The content of the talk did not rise above the mental level of the "communications." The tone of the voice was somewhat forced, and only became natural when, in the course of the talk, the voice approximated to the medium's own.

(In later sittings the voice was only altered for a few moments when a new spirit manifested itself.)

Afterwards there was amnesia for the trance-conversation. She gave hints about a sojourn in the other world, and she spoke of an undreamed-of blessedness which she felt.

It must be further noted that her conversation in the attack occurred quite spontaneously, and was not in response to any suggestions.

Directly after this séance S. W. became acquainted with the book of Justinus Kerner, *Die Seherin von Prevorst*. She began thereupon to magnetise herself towards the end of the attack, partly by means of regular passes, partly by curious circles and figures of eight, which she described symmetrically with both arms. She did this, she said, to disperse the severe headaches which occurred after the attacks. In the August séances, not detailed here, there were in addition to the grandfather numerous spirits of other relatives who did not produce anything very remarkable. Each time when a new one came on the scene the movement of the glass was changed in a striking way; it generally ran along the rows of letters, touching one or other of them, but no sense could be made of it. The orthography was very uncertain and arbitrary, and the first sentences were frequently incomprehensible or broken up into a meaningless medley of letters. Generally automatic writing suddenly began at this point. Sometimes automatic writing was attempted during complete darkness. The movements began with violent backward jerks of the whole arm, so that the paper was pierced by the pencil. The first attempt at writing consisted of numerous strokes and zigzag lines about 8 cm. high. In later attempts there came first unreadable words, in large handwriting, which gradually became smaller and clearer. It was not essentially different from the medium's own. The grandfather was again the controlling spirit.

V. Somnambulic attacks in September, 1899. S. W. sits upon the sofa, leans back, shuts her eyes, breathes lightly and regularly. She gradually becomes cataleptic, the catalepsy disappears after about two minutes, when she lies in an apparently quiet sleep with complete muscular relaxation. She suddenly begins to speak in a subdued voice: "No! you take the red, I'll take the white, you can take the green, and you the blue. Are you ready? We will go now." (A pause of several minutes during which her face assumes a corpse-like pallor. Her hands feel cold and are very bloodless.) She suddenly calls out with a loud, solemn voice: "Albert, Albert, Albert," then whispering: "Now you speak," followed by a longer pause, when the pallor of the face attains the highest possible degree. Again, in a loud solemn voice, "Albert, Albert, do you not believe your father? I tell you many errors are contained in N.'s teaching. Think about it." Pause. The pallor of the face decreases. "He's very frightened. He could not speak any more." (These words in her usual conversational tone.) Pause. "He will certainly think about it," S. W. now speaks again in the same tone, in a strange idiom which sounds like French or Italian, now recalling the former, now the latter. She speaks fluently, rapidly, and with charm. It is possible to understand a few words but not to remember the whole, because the language is so strange. From time-to-time words recur, *wena, wenes, wenai, wene,* ect. The absolute naturalness of the proceedings is bewildering. From time to time she pauses as if some one were answering her. Suddenly she speaks in German, "Is time already up?" (In a troubled voice.) "Must I go already? Goodbye, goodbye." With the last words there passes over her face an indescribable expression of ecstatic blessedness. She raises her arms, opens her eyes,—hitherto closed,—looks radiantly upwards. She remains a moment thus, then her arms sink slackly, her eyes shut, the expression of her face is tired and exhausted. After a short cataleptic stage she awakes with a sigh. She looks around astonished: "I've slept again, haven't I?" She is told she has been talking during the sleep, whereupon she becomes much annoyed, and this increases when she learns she has spoken in a foreign tongue. "But didn't I tell the spirits I don't want it? It mustn't be. It exhausts me too much." Begins to cry. "Oh, God! Oh, God! must then everything, everything, come back again like last time? Is

nothing spared me?" The next day at the same
time there was another attack. When S. W.
has fallen asleep Ulrich von Gerbenstein suddenly announces himself. He is an entertain-
ing chatterer, speaks very fluently in high
German with a North-German accent. Asked
what S. W. is now doing, after much circum-
locution he explains that she is far away, and
he is meanwhile here to look after her body,
the circulation of the blood, the respiration,
etc. He must take care that meanwhile no
black person takes possession of her and
harms her. Upon urgent questioning he re-
lates that S. W. has gone with the others to
Japan, to appear to a distant relative and to
restrain him from a stupid marriage. He then
announces in a whisper the exact moment
when the manifestation takes place. Forbid-
den any conversation for a few minutes, he
points to the sudden pallor occurring in S. W.,
remarking that materialisation at such a great
distance is at the cost of correspondingly great
force. He then orders cold bandages to the
head to alleviate the severe headache which
would occur afterwards. As the colour of the
face gradually becomes more natural the conversation grows livelier. All kinds of childish
jokes and trivialities are uttered; suddenly U.
von G. says, "I see them coming, but they are
still very far off; I see them there like a star."
S. W. points to the North. We are naturally

astonished, and ask why they do not come from the East, whereto U. von G. laughingly retorts: "Oh, but they come the direct way over the North Pole. I am going now; farewell." Immediately after S. W. sighs, wakes up, is ill-tempered, complains of extremely bad headache. She saw U. von G. standing by her body; what had he told us? She gets angry about the "silly chatter" from which he cannot refrain.

VI. Begins in the usual way. Extreme pallor; lies stretched out, scarcely breathing. Speaks suddenly, with loud, solemn voice: "Yes, be frightened; I am; I warn you against N.'s teaching. See, in hope is everything that belongs to faith. You would like to know who I am. God gives where one least expects it. Do you not know me?" Then unintelligible whispering; after a few minutes she awakes.

VII. S. W. soon falls asleep; lies stretched out on the sofa. Is very pale. Says nothing, sighs deeply from time to time. Casts up her eyes, rises, sits on the sofa, bends forward, speaks softly: "You have sinned grievously, have fallen far." Bends forward still, as if speaking to some one who kneels before her. She stands up, turns to the right, stretches out her hands, and points to the spot over which she has been bending. "Will you forgive her?" she asks, loudly. "Do not forgive men, but their spirits. Not she, but her human body has sinned." Then she kneels down, remains quite still for about ten minutes in the attitude of prayer. Then she gets up suddenly, looks to heaven with ecstatic expression, and then throws herself again on her knees, with her face bowed on her hands, whispering incomprehensible words. She remains rigid in this position several minutes. Then she gets up, looks again upwards with a radiant countenance, and lies down on the sofa; soon after she wakes.

III

DEVELOPMENT OF THE
SOMNAMBULIC PERSONALITIES

AT the beginning of many séances the glass
was allowed to move by itself, when occasionally the advice followed in stereotyped fashion: "You must ask."

Since convinced spiritualists took part in
the séances, all kinds of spiritualistic wonders
were of course demanded, and especially the
"protecting spirits." In reply, sometimes
names of well-known dead people were produced, and other times they were unknown
names, *e.g.* Berthe de Valours, Elizabeth von
Thierfelsenburg, Ulrich von Gerbenstein, etc.
The controlling spirit was almost without exception the medium's grandfather, who once
explained: "he loved her more than any one in
this world because he had protected her from
childhood up, and knew all her thoughts."
This personality produced a flood of Biblical
maxims, edifying observations, and song-
book verses; the following is a specimen:—

> *In true believing,*
> *To faith in God cling ever nigh,*
> *Thy heavenly comfort never leaving,*
> *Which having, man can never die.*
> *Refuge in God is peace for ever,*

When earthly cares oppress the mind;
Who from the heart can pray is never
Bowed down by fate, howe'er un. kind.

Numerous similar elaborations betrayed
by their banal, unctuous contents their origin
in some tract or other. When S. W. had to
speak in ecstasy, lively dialogues developed
between the circle-members and the somnambulic personality. The content of the answers
received is essentially just the same common-
place edifying stuff as that of the psycho-
graphic communications. The character of
this personality is distinguished by its dry and
tedious solemnity, rigorous conventionality
and pietistic virtue (which is not consistent
with the historic reality). The grandfather is
the medium's guide and protector. During the
ecstatic state he gives all kinds of advice,
prophesies later attacks and the visions she
will see on waking, etc. He orders cold bandages, gives directions concerning the medium's lying down or the date of the séances.
His relationship to the medium is an extremely tender one. In liveliest contrast to this
heavy dream-person stands a personality, ap-
pearing first sporadically, in the psycho-
graphic communications of the first séance. It
soon disclosed itself as the dead brother of a
Mr. R., who was then taking part in the séance. This dead brother, Mr. P. R., was full of

commonplaces about brotherly love towards his living brother. He evaded particular questions in all manner of ways. But he developed a quite astonishing eloquence towards the ladies of the circle and in particular offered his allegiance to one whom Mr. P. R. had never known when alive. He affirmed that he had already cared very much for her in his lifetime, had often met her in the street without knowing who she was, and was now uncommonly delighted to become acquainted with her in this unusual manner. With such insipid compliments, scornful remarks to the men, harmless childish jokes, etc., he took up a large part of the séance. Several of the members found fault with the frivolity and banality of this "spirit," whereupon he disappeared for one or two séances, but soon reappeared, at first well-behaved, often indeed uttering Christian maxims, but soon dropping back into the old tone. Besides these two sharply differentiated personalities, others appeared who varied but little from the grandfather's type; they were mostly dead relatives of the medium. The general atmosphere of the first two months' séances was accordingly solemnly edifying, disturbed only from time to time by Mr. P. R.'s trivial chatter. Some weeks after the beginning of the séances, Mr. R. left our circle, whereupon a remarkable change took place in Mr. P. R.'s conversation.

He became monosyllabic, came less often, and after a few séances vanished altogether, later on he reappeared but with great infrequency, and for the most part only when the medium was alone with the particular lady mentioned. Then a new personality forced himself into the foreground; in contrast to Mr. P. R., who always spoke the Swiss dialect, this gentleman adopted an affected North-German way of speaking. In all else he was an exact copy of Mr. P. R. His eloquence was somewhat remarkable, since S. W. had only a very scanty knowledge of high German, whilst this new personality, who called himself Ulrich von Gerbenstein, spoke an almost faultless German, rich in charming phrases and compliments.[°]

Ulrich von Gerbenstein was a witty chatterer, full of repartee, an idler, a great admirer of the ladies, frivolous, and most superficial.

During the winter of 1899-1900 he gradually came to dominate the situation more and more, and took over one by one all the above-mentioned functions of the grandfather, so that under his influence the serious character of the séances disappeared.

All suggestions to the contrary proved unavailing, and at last the séances had on this

---

[°] It must be noted that a frequent guest in S. W.'s home was a gentleman who spoke high German.

account to be suspended for longer and longer intervals. There is a peculiarity common to all these somnambulic personalities which must be noted. They have access to the medium's memory, even to the unconscious portion, they are also *au courant* with the visions which she has in the ecstatic state, *but they have only the most superficial knowledge of her phantasies during the ecstasy*. Of the somnambulic dreams they know only what they occasionally pick up from the members of the circle. On doubtful points they can give no information, or only such as contradicts the medium's explanations. The stereotyped answer to these questions runs: "Ask Ivenes."° "Ivenes knows." From the examples given of different ecstatic moments it is clear that the medium's consciousness is by no means idle during the trance, but develops a striking and multiplex phantastic activity. For the reconstruction of S. W.'s somnambulic self we have to depend altogether upon her several statements; for in the first place her spontaneous utterances connecting her with the waking self are few, and often irrelevant, and in the second very many of these ecstatic states go by without gesture, and without speech, so that no conclusions as to the inner happenings can

---

° Ivenes is the mystical name of the medium's somnambulic self.

afterwards be drawn from the external appearances. S. W. is almost totally amnesic for the automatic phenomena during ecstasy as far as they come within the territory of the new personalities of her ego. Of all the other phenomena, such as loud talking, babbling, etc., which are directly connected with her own ego she usually has a clear remembrance. But in every case there is complete amnesia only during the first few minutes after the ecstasy. Within the first half-hour, during which there usually prevails a kind of semi-somnambulism with a dreamlike manner, hallucinations, etc., the amnesia gradually disappears, whilst fragmentary memories emerge of what has occurred, but in a quite irregular and arbitrary fashion.

The later séances were usually begun by our hands being joined and laid on the table, whereon the table at once began to move. Meanwhile S. W. gradually became somnambulic, took her hands from the table, lay back on the sofa, and fell into the ecstatic sleep. She sometimes related her experiences to us afterwards, but showed herself very reticent if strangers were present. After the very first ecstasy she indicated that she played a distinguished *rôle* among the spirits. She had a special name, as had each of the spirits; hers was *Ivenes*; her grandfather looked after her with particular care. In the ecstasy with the flower-

vision we learnt her special secret, hidden till
then beneath the deepest silence. During the
séances in which her spirit spoke she made
long journeys, mostly to relatives, to whom
she said she appeared, or she found herself on
the Other Side, in "That space between the
stars which people think is empty, but in
which there are really very many spirit-
worlds." In the semi-somnambulic state which
frequently followed her attacks, she once described, in peculiar poetic fashion, a land-
scape on the Other Side, "a wondrous, moon-
lit valley, set aside for the races not yet born."
She represented her somnambulic ego as being almost completely released from the body.
It is a fully-grown but small, black-haired
woman, of pronounced Jewish type, clothed
in white garments, her head covered with a
turban. She understands and speaks the language of the spirits, "for spirits still, from old
human custom, do speak to one another, although they do not really need to, since they
mutually understand one another's thoughts."
She "does not really always talk with the spirits, but just looks at them, and so understands
their thoughts." She travels in the company of
four or five spirits, dead relatives, and visits
her living relatives and acquaintances in order
to investigate their life and their way of thinking; she further visits all places which
lie within the radius of these spectral

inhabitants. From her acquaintanceship with Kerner's book, she discovered and improved upon the ideas of the black spirits who are kept enchanted in certain places, or exist partly beneath the earth's surface (compare the *Seherin von Prevorst*). This activity caused her much trouble and pain; in and after the ecstasy she complained of suffocating feelings, violent headache, etc. But every fortnight, on Wednesdays, she could pass the whole night in the garden on the Other Side in the company of holy spirits. There she was taught everything concerning the forces of the world, the endless complicated relationships and affinities of human beings, and all besides about the laws of reincarnation, the inhabitants of the stars, etc. Unfortunately only the system of the world-forces and reincarnation achieved any expression. As to the other matters she only let fall disconnected observations. For example, once she returned from a railway journey in an extremely disturbed state. It was thought at first something unpleasant had happened, till she managed to compose herself, and said, "A star-inhabitant had sat opposite to her in the train." From the description which she gave of this being, I recognised a well-known elderly merchant I happened to know, who has a rather unsympathetic face. In connection with this experience she related all kinds of peculiarities of these

star-dwellers; they have no god-like souls, as
men have, they pursue no science, no philosophy, but in technical arts they are far more ad-
vanced than men. Thus on Mars a flying-machine has long been in existence; the whole of
Mars is covered with canals, these canals are
cleverly excavated lakes and serve for irriga-
tion. The canals are quite superficial; the water in them is very shallow. The excavating
caused the inhabitants of Mars no particular
trouble, for the soil there is lighter than the
Earth's. The canals are nowhere bridged, but
that does not prevent communication, for everything travels by flying-machine. Wars no
longer occur on the stars, for no differences of
opinion exist. The star-dwellers have not human bodies, but the most laughable ones possible, such as one would never imagine. Human spirits who are allowed to travel on the
Other Side may not set foot on the stars.
Equally, wandering star-dwellers may not
come to the earth, but must remain at a distance of twenty-five metres above the earth's
surface. Should they transgress they remain in
the power of the earth, and must assume human bodies, and are only set free again after
their natural death. As men, they are cold,
hard-hearted, cruel. S. W. recognises them by
a singular expression in which the "Spiritual"
is lacking, and by their hairless, eyebrowless,

sharply-cut faces. Napoleon was a star-dweller.

In her journeys she does not see the places through which she hastens. She has a feeling of floating, and the spirits tell her when she is at the right spot. Then, as a rule, she only sees the face and upper part of the person to whom she is supposed to appear, or whom she wishes to see. She can seldom say in what kind of surroundings she sees this person. Occasionally she saw me, but only my head without any surroundings. She occupied herself much with the enchanting of spirits, and for this purpose she wrote oracular sayings in a foreign tongue, on slips of paper which she concealed in all sorts of queer places. An Italian murderer, presumably living in my house, and whom she called Conventi, was specially displeasing to her. She tried several times to cast a spell upon him, and without my knowledge hid several papers about, on which messages were written; these were later found by chance. One such, written in red ink, was as follows:

Conventi
Marche. 4 govi
Ivenes.
Conventi, go
orden, Astaf
vent.
Gen palus, vent allis
ton prost afta ben genallis.

Unfortunately, I never obtained any interpretation of this. S. W. was quite inaccessible in this matter. Occasionally the somnambulic Ivenes speaks directly to the public. She does so in dignified fashion, rather precociously, but she is not wearisomely unctuous and impossibly twaddling as are her two guides; she is a serious, mature person, devout and pious, full of womanly tenderness and great modesty, always yielding to the judgments of others. This expression of plaintive emotion and melancholy resignation is peculiar to her. She looks beyond this world, and unwillingly returns to reality; she bemoans her hard lot, and her unsympathetic family surroundings. Associated with this there is something elevated about her; she commands her spirits, despises the twaddling chatter of Gerbenstein, consoles others, directs those in distress, warns and protects them from dangers to body and soul. She is the intermediary for the entire intellectual output of all manifestations, but she herself ascribes it to the direction of the spirits. It is Ivenes who entirely controls S. W.'s semi-somnambulic state.

In semi-somnambulism S. W. gave some of those taking part in the séances the opportunity to compare her with the *Seherin von Prevorst* (Prophetess of Prevorst). This suggestion was not without results. S. W. gave hints of earlier existences which she had already

lived through, and after a few weeks she suddenly disclosed a whole system of reincarnations, although she had never before mentioned anything of the kind. Ivenes is a spiritual being who is something more than the
spirits of other human beings. Every human
spirit must incorporate himself twice in the
course of the centuries. But Ivenes must incorporate herself at least once every two hun-
dred years; besides herself only two other persons have participated in this fate, namely,
Swedenborg and Miss Florence Cook
(Crookes's famous medium). S. W. calls these
two personages her brother and sister. She
gave no information about their pre-existences. In the beginning of the nineteenth century Ivenes was Frau Hauffe, the Prophetess
of Prevorst; at the end of the eighteenth century, a clergyman's wife in central Germany (locality unknown). As the latter she
was seduced by Goethe and bore him a child.
In the fifteenth century she was a Saxon coun-
tess, and had the poetic name of Thierfelsenburg. Ulrich von Gerbenstein is a relative
from that line. The interval of 300 years, and
her adventure with Goethe, must be atoned
for by the sorrows of the Prophetess of Prevorst. In the thirteenth century she was a no-
blewoman of Southern France, called de Valours, and was burnt as a witch. From the thirteenth century to the Christian persecution

under Nero there were numerous reincarnations of which S. W. could give no detailed account. In the Christian persecution under Nero she played a martyr's part. Then comes a period of obscurity till the time of David, when Ivenes was an ordinary Jewess. After her death she received from Astaf, an angel from a high heaven, the mandate for her future wonderful career. In all her pre-existences she was a medium and an intermediary in the intercourse between this side and the other. Her brothers and sisters are equally old and have the like vocation. In her various pre-existences she was sometimes married, and in this way gradually founded a whole system of relationships with whose endless complicated inter-relations she occupied herself in many ecstasies. Thus, for example, about the eighth century she was the mother of her earthly father and, moreover, of her grandfather, and mine. Hence the striking friendship of these two old gentlemen, otherwise strangers. As Mme. de Valours she was the present writer's mother. When she was burnt as a witch the writer took it much to heart, and went into a cloister at Rouen, wore a grey habit, became Prior, wrote a work on Botany and died at over eighty years of age. In the refectory of the cloister there hung a picture of Mme. de Valours, in which she was depicted in a half-reclining position. (S. W. in the semi-somnambulic state often took this position on the sofa. It corresponds exactly to that of Mme. Recamier in David's well-known picture.) A gentleman who often took part in the séances, who had some slight resemblance to the writer, was also one of her sons from that period. Around this core of relationship there grouped themselves, more or less intimately connected, all the persons in any way related or known to her. One came from the fifteenth century, another—a cousin—from the eighteenth century, and so on.

From the three great family stocks grew by far the greater part of the present European peoples. She and her brothers and sisters are descended from Adam, who arose by materialisation; the other then-existing families, from whom Cain took his wife, were descended from apes. S. W. produced from this circle of relationship an extensive family-gossip, a very flood of romantic stories, piquant adventures, etc. Sometimes the target of her romances was a lady acquaintance of the writer's who for some undiscoverable reason was peculiarly antipathetic to her. She declared that this lady was an incarnation of a celebrated Parisian poisoner, who had achieved great notoriety in the eighteenth century. She maintained that this lady still continued her dangerous work, but in a much more ingenious way than formerly; through the inspiration of the wicked spirits who accompany her she had discovered a liquid which when merely exposed to the air attracted tubercle bacilli and formed a splendid developing medium for them. By means of this liquid, which she was wont to mix with the food, the lady had brought about the death of her husband (who had indeed died of tuberculosis); also one of her lovers, and of her own brother, for the sake of his inheritance. Her eldest son was an illegitimate child by her lover. As a widow she had secretly borne to another lover an illegitimate child, and finally she had had an unnatural relationship with her own brother (who was later on poisoned). In this way S. W. spun innumerable stories, in which she believed quite implicitly. The persons of these stories appeared in the drama of her visions, as did the lady before referred to, going through the pantomime of making confession and receiving absolution of sins. Everything interesting occurring in her surroundings was incorporated in this system of romances, and given an order in the network of relationships with a more or less exact statement as to their pre-existences and the spirits influencing them. It fared thus with all who made S. W.'s acquaintance: they were valued at a second or first incarnation, according as they possessed a marked or indefinite character. They were generally described as

relatives, and always exactly in the same definite way. Only subsequently, often several
weeks later, after an ecstasy, there would
make its appearance a new complicated ro-
mance which explained the striking relationship through pre-existences or through illegitimate relations. Persons sympathetic to S. W.
were usually very near relatives. Most of these
family romances were very carefully made up,
so that to contradict them was impossible.
They were always worked out with a quite bewildering certainty, and surprised one by an
extremely clever evaluation of certain details
which she had noticed or taken from somewhere. For the most part the romances had a
ghastly character, murder by poison and dag-
ger, seduction and divorce, forgery of wills,
played the chief role.

Mystic Science. — In reference to scientific
questions S. W. put forward numerous suggestions. Generally towards the end of the séances there was talk and debate about various
subjects of scientific and spiritistic nature. S.
W. never took part in the discussion, but generally sat dreamily in a corner in a semi-somnambulic state. She listened to one and another, taking hold of the talk in a half-dream,
but she could never relate anything connect-
edly; if asked about it only partial explanations were given. In the course of the winter
hints emerged in various séances: "The spirits

taught her about the world-forces and the strange revelations from the other side, yet she would not tell anything now." Once she tried to give a description, but only said: "On one side was the light, on the other the power of attraction." Finally, in March 1900, when for some time nothing had been heard of the teachings at the séances, she announced suddenly with a joyful face that she had now received everything from the spirits. She drew out a long narrow strip of paper upon which were numerous names. Although I asked for it she would not let it leave her hands, but dictated the following scheme to me (*See Fig. 1*):

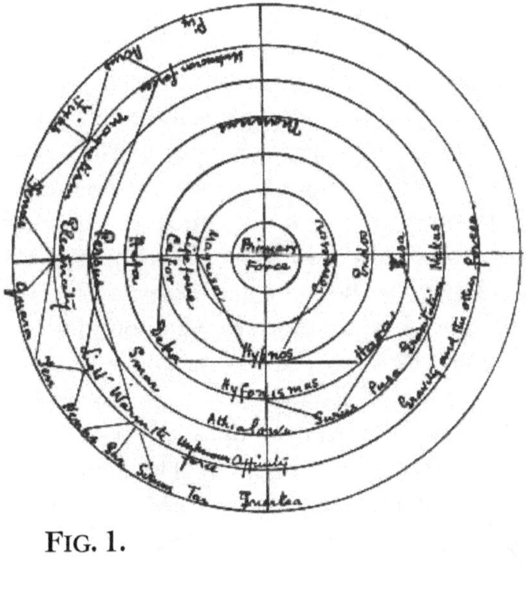

FIG. 1.

I can remember clearly that in the course of the winter of 1895 we spoke several times in S. W.'s presence of the forces of attraction and repulsion in connection with Kant's "Natural History of the Heavens"; we spoke also of the "Law of the Conservation of Energy," of the different forces of energy, and of the question whether the force of gravity was perhaps a form of movement. From this talk S. W. had plainly created the foundation of her mystic system. She gave the following explanation: The natural forces are arranged in seven circles. Outside these circles are three more, in which unknown forces intermediate between energy and matter are found. Matter is found in seven circles which surround ten inner ones. In the centre stands the primary force, which is the original cause of creation and is a spiritual force. The first circle which surrounds the primary force is matter which is not really a force and does not arise from the primary force, but it unites with the primary force and from this union the first descendants are the spiritual forces; on the one hand the Good or Light Powers, on the other the Dark Powers. The Power Magnesor consists most of primary force; the Power Connesor, in which the dark might of matter is greatest, contains the least. The further outwards the primary force streams forth, the weaker it becomes, but weaker too becomes

the power of matter, since its power is greatest
where the collision with the primary power is
most violent, *i.e.* in the Power Connesor.
Within the circles there are fresh analogous
forces of equal strength but making in the opposite direction. The system can also be described in a single series beginning with primary force, Magnesor, Cafor, etc., proceeding
from left to right on the scheme and ascending
with Tusa, Endos, ending with Connesor;
only then the survey of the grade of intensity
is made more difficult. Every force in the
outer circle is combined from the nearest adjacent forces of the inner circle.

1. *The Magnesor Group.* — The so-called
powers of Light descend in direct line from
Magnesor, but slightly influenced by the dark
side. The powers Magnesor and Cafor form
together the so-called Life Force, which is no
single power but is differently combined in
animals and plants. Between Magnesor and
Cafor there exists the Life Force of Man.
Morally good men and those mediums who
bring about interviews of good spirits on the
earth have most Magnesor. Somewhere about
the middle there stand the life forces of animals, and in Cafor that of plants. Nothing is
known about Hefa, or rather S. W. can give
no information. Persus is the fundamental
power which comes to light in the phenomenon of the forces of locomotion. Its

recognisable forces are Warmth, Light, Electricity, Magnetism, and two unknown forces, one of which only exists in comets. Of the powers of the seventh circle S. W. could only point out north and south magnetism and positive and negative electricity. *Deka* is unknown. *Smar* is of peculiar significance, to be indicated below; it leads to—

2 *Group Hypnos and Hypnotisms* are powers which only dwell within certain beings, in those who are in a position to exert a magnetic influence upon others. *Athialowi* is the sexual instinct. Chemical affinity is directly derived from it. In the ninth circle under it arises indolence (that is the line of *Smar*). *Svens* and *kara* are of unknown significance. *Pusa* corresponds to *smar* in the opposite sense.

3. *The Connesor Group.*— Connesor is the opposite pole of Magnesor. It is the dark and wicked power equal in intensity to the good power of light. While the good power creates, this one turns into the opposite. Endos is an elemental power of minerals. From these (significance unknown) gravitation proceeds, which on its side is designated as the elemental force of the forces of resistance that occur in phenomena (gravity, capillarity, adhesion and cohesion). Nakus is the secret power of a rare stone which controls the effect of snake poison. The two powers *Smar* and *pusa* have a special importance. According to S. W.,

ɔmar develops in the bodies of morally good men at the moment of death. This power enables the soul to rise to the powers of light. *Pusa* behaves in the opposite way, for it is the power which conducts morally bad people to the dark side in the state of Connesor.

In the sixth circle the visible world begins, which only appears to be so sharply divided from the other side in consequence of the fickleness of our organs of sense. In reality the transition is a very gradual one, and there are people who live on a higher stage of knowledge because their perceptions and sensations are more delicate than those of others. Great seers are enabled to see manifestations of force where ordinary people can perceive nothing. S. W. sees Magnesor as a white or bluish vapour, which chiefly develops when good spirits are near. Connesor is a dark vapour-like fluid, which, like Magnesor, develops on the appearance of "black" spirits. For instance, the night before the beginning of great visions the shiny vapour of Magnesor spreads in thick layers, out of which, the good spirits grow to visible white forces. It is just the same with Connesor. But these powers have their different mediums. S. W. is a Magnesor medium, as were the Prophetess of Prevorst and Swedenborg. The materialisation mediums of the spiritualists are mostly Connesor mediums, because materialisation takes place much more easily through Connesor on account of its close connection with the properties of matter. In the summer of 1900 S. W. tried several times to produce the circles of matter, but she never arrived at other than vague and incomprehensible hints and afterwards spoke no more about this.

Conclusion — The really interesting and valuable séances came to an end with the production of the system of powers. Before this a gradual decline in the vividness of the ecstasies was noticeable. Ulrich von Gerbenstein came increasingly to the front, and filled up the séances with his childish chatter. The visions which S. W. had in the meantime likewise seem to have lost vividness and plasticity of formation, for S. W. was afterwards only able to feel pleasant sensations in the presence of good spirits, and disagreeableness in that of bad spirits. Nothing new was produced. There was something of uncertainty in the trance talks, as if feeling and seeking for the impression which she was making upon the audience, together with an increasing staleness in the content. In the outward behaviour of S. W. there arose also a marked shyness and uncertainty, so that the impression of wilful deception became ever stronger. The writer therefore soon withdrew from the séances. S. W. experimented afterwards in other circles, and six months after my leaving was caught cheating *in flagranti delicto*. She wanted to arouse again by spiritualistic experiments the lost belief in her supernatural powers; she concealed small objects in her dress, throwing them up in the air during the dark séance. With this her part was played out. Since then, eighteen months have passed during which I have not seen S. W. I have learnt from an observer who knew her in the earlier days, that she has now and again strange states of short duration during which she is very pale and silent, and has a fixed glittering look. I did not hear any more of visions. She is said not to take part any longer in spiritualistic séances. S. W. is now in a large business, and according to all accounts is an industrious and responsible person who does her work eagerly and cleverly, giving entire satisfaction. According to the account of trustworthy persons, her character has much improved; she has become quieter, more regular and sympathetic. No other abnormalities have appeared in her. This case, in spite of its incompleteness, contains a mass of psychological problems whose exposition goes far beyond the limits of this little work. We must therefore be satisfied with a mere sketch of the various striking manifestations. For the sake of a more lucid exposition it seems better to review the various states separately.

1. *The Waking State.* — Here the patient shows various peculiarities. As we have seen, at school she was often distracted, lost herself in a peculiar way, was moody; her behaviour changes inconsequently, now quiet, shy, reserved, now lively, noisy and talkative. She cannot be called unintelligent, but she strikes one sometimes as narrow-minded, sometimes as having isolated intelligent moments. Her memory is good on the whole, but owing to her distraction it is much impaired. Thus, despite much discussion and reading of Kerner's "Seherin von Prevorst," for many weeks, she does not know, if directly asked, whether the author's name is *Koerner* or *Kerner*, nor the name of the Prophetess. All the same, when it occasionally comes up, the name *Kerner* is correctly written in the automatic communications. In general it may be said that her character has something extremely impulsive, incomprehensible, protean. Deducting the want of balance due to puberty, there remains a pathological residue which expresses itself in reactions which follow no rule and a bizarre unaccountable character. This character may be called *déséquilibré*, or unstable. Its specific mould is derived from traits which can certainly be regarded as hysterical. This is decidedly so in the conditions of distraction. As

Janet[*] maintains, the foundation of hysterical anæsthesia is the loss of attention. He was able to prove in youthful hysterics "a striking indifference and distracted attention in the whole region of the emotional life." Misreading is a notable instance, which beautifully illustrates hysterical dispersion of attention. The psychology of this process may perhaps be viewed as follows: during reading aloud attention becomes paralysed for this act and is directed towards some other object. Meanwhile the reading is continued mechanically, the sense impressions are received as before, but in consequence of the dispersion the excitability of the perceptive centre is lowered, so that the strength of the sense impression is no longer adequate to fix the attention in such a way that perception as such is conducted along the motor speech route; thus all the inflowing associations which at once unite with any new sense impression are repressed. The further psychological mechanism permits of only two possible explanations: (1) The admission of the sense impression is received unconsciously (because of the increase of threshold stimulus), in the perceptive centre just below the threshold of consciousness, and consequently is not incorporated in the attention

[*] "The Major Symptoms of Hysteria." New York: The Macmillan Company.

and conducted back to the speech route. It only reaches verbal expression through the intervention of the nearest associations, in our case through the dialect expression for the object. (2) The sense impression is perceived consciously, but at the moment of its entrance into the speech route it reaches a territory whose excitability is diminished by the dispersion of attention. At this place the dialect word is substituted by association for the motor speech image, and it is uttered as such. In either case it is certain that it is the acoustic dispersed attention which fails to correct the error. Which of the two explanations is correct cannot be proved in this case; probably both approach the truth, for the dispersion of attention seems to be general, and in each case concerns more than one of the centres engaged in the act of reading aloud. In our case this phenomenon has a special value, for we have here a quite elementary automatic phenomenon. It may be called hysterical in so far as in this concrete case a state of exhaustion and intoxication, with its parallel manifestations, can be excluded. A healthy person only exceptionally allows himself to be so engaged by an object that he fails to correct the errors of a dispersed attention—those of the kind described. The frequency of these occurrences in the patient point to a considerable limitation of the field of consciousness, in so far as she can only master a relative minimum of elementary sensations flowing in at the same time. If we wish to describe more exactly the psychological state of the "psychic shady side," we might call it either a sleeping or a dream-state, according as passivity or activity predominated. There is, at all events, a pathological dream-state of very rudimentary extension and intensity and its genesis is spontaneous; dream-states arising spontaneously, with the production of automatisms, are generally regarded as hysterical on the whole. It must be pointed out that these instances of misreading occurred frequently in our subject, and that the term hysterical is employed in this sense; so far as we know, it is only on a foundation of hysterical constitution that spontaneous states of partial sleep or dreams occur frequently.

Binet° has studied experimentally the automatic substitution of some adjacent association in his hysterics. If he pricked the anæsthetic hand of the patient without his noticing the prick, he thought of "points"; if the anæsthetic finger was moved, he thought of "sticks" or "columns." When the anæsthetic hand, concealed from the patient's sight by a screen, writes "Salpêtrière," she sees in front of her the word "Salpêtrière" in white writing

---

° Binet, "Les altérations de la personnalité."

on a black ground. This recalls the experiments above referred to of Guinon and Sophie Waltke.

We thus find in our subject, at a time when there was nothing to indicate the later phenomena, rudimentary automatisms, fragments of dream manifestations, which imply in themselves the possibility that some day more than one association would creep in between the perception of the dispersed attention and consciousness. The misreading shows us, moreover, a certain automatic independence of the psychical elements. This occasionally expands to a more or less fleeting dispersion of attention, although with very slight results which are never in any way striking or suspicious; this dispersedness approximates to that of the physiological dream. The misreading can be thus conceived as a prodromal symptom of the later events; especially as its psychology is prototypical for the mechanism of somnambulic dreams, which are indeed nothing but a many-sided multiplication and manifold variation of the elementary processes reviewed above. I never succeeded in demonstrating during my observations similar rudimentary automatisms. It would seem that in course of time the states of dispersed attention, to a certain extent beneath the surface of consciousness, at first of low degree have grown into these remarkable somnambulic attacks; hence they disappeared during the waking state, which was free from attacks. So far as concerns the development of the patient's character, beyond a certain not very extensive ripening, no remarkable change could be demonstrated during the observations lasting nearly two years. More remarkable is the fact that in the two years since the cessation (complete?) of the somnambulic attacks, a considerable change in character has taken place. We shall have occasion later on to speak of the importance of this observation.

Semi-somnambulism. — In S. W.'s case the following condition was indicated by the term semi-somnambulism. For some time after and before the actual somnambulic attack the patient finds herself in a state whose most salient feature can best be described as "preoccupation." She only lends half an ear to the conversation around her, answers at random, often gets absorbed in all manner of hallucinations; her face is solemn, her look ecstatic, visionary, ardent. Closer observation discloses a far-reaching alteration of the entire character. She is now serious, dignified; when she speaks her subject is always an extremely serious one. In this condition she can talk so seriously, forcibly and convincingly, that one is tempted to ask oneself if this is really a girl of fifteen and a half. One has the impression of a mature woman possessed of considerable dramatic talent. The reason for this seriousness, this solemnity of behaviour, is given in her explanation that at these times she stands at the frontier of this world and the other, and associates just as truly with the spirits of the dead as with living people. And, indeed, her conversation is usually divided between answers to real objective questions and hallucinatory ones. I call this state semi-somnambulism.

IV

AUTOMATISMS

SEMI-SOMNAMBULISM is characterised by the continuity of consciousness with that of the waking state and by the appearance of various automatisms which give evidence of an activity of the subconscious self, independent of that of consciousness.

Our case shows the following automatic phenomena:

(1) Automatic movements of the table.

(2) Automatic writing.

(3) Hallucinations.

1. *Automatic movements of the table* — Before the patient came under my observation she had been influenced by the suggestion of "table-turning," which she had first come across as a game. As soon as she entered the circle there appeared communications from members of her family which showed her to be a medium. I could only find out that, as soon as ever her hand was placed on the table, the typical movements began. The resulting communications have no interest for us. But the automatic character of the act itself deserves some discussion, for we may, without more ado, set aside the imputation that there was

any question of intentional and voluntary pushing or pulling on the part of the patient.

As we know from the investigations of Chevreul,° Gley, Lehmann and others, unconscious motor phenomena are not only of frequent occurrence among hysterical persons, and those pathologically inclined in other directions, but they are also relatively easily produced in normal persons who show no other spontaneous automatisms. I have made many experiments on these lines, and can confirm this observation. In the great majority of instances all that is required is enough patience to put up with an hour of quiet waiting. In most subjects, motor automatisms will be obtained in a more or less high degree if contra-suggestions do not intervene as obstacles. In a relatively small percentage the phenomena arise spontaneously, *i.e.* directly under the influence of verbal suggestion or of some earlier auto-suggestion. In this instance the case is powerfully affected by suggestion. In general, the particular predisposition is subject to all those laws which also hold good for normal hypnosis. Nevertheless, certain special circumstances are to be taken into account, conditioned by the peculiarity of the case. It is not a question of a total hypnosis,

---

° Complete references in Binet, *"Les altérations,"* p. 197, footnote.

but of a partial one, limited entirely to the motor area of the arm, like the cerebral anæsthesia produced by "magnetic passes" for a painful spot in the body. We touch the spot in question employing verbal suggestion or making use of some existing auto-suggestion, using the tactile stimulus which we know acts suggestively, to bring about the desired partial hypnosis. In accordance with this procedure, refractory subjects can be brought easily enough to an exhibition of automatism. The experimenter intentionally gives the table a slight push, or, better, a series of rhythmic but very slight taps. After a short time he notices that the oscillations become stronger, that they continue although he has interrupted his own intentional movements. The experiment has succeeded, the subject has unsuspectingly taken up the suggestion. By this procedure much more is obtained than by verbal suggestion. In very receptive persons and in all those cases where movement seems to arise spontaneously, the purposeful tremulous movements,° not perceptible by the subject, assume

---

° As is known, during the waking-state the hands and arms are never quite still, but are constantly subjected to fine tremors. Preyer, Lehmann, and others have proved that these movements are influenced in a high degree by the predominant presentations. Preyer shows that the outstretched

the *rôle* of *agent provocateur*. In this way persons who, by themselves, have never obtained automatic movements of a coarse calibre, sometimes assume the unconscious guidance of the table-movements, provided that the tremors are strong and that the medium understands their meaning. In this case the medium takes control of the slight oscillations and returns them considerably strengthened, but rarely at exactly the same instant, generally a few seconds later, in this way revealing the agent's conscious or unconscious thought. By means of this simple mechanism there may arise those cases of thought-reading so bewildering at first sight. A very simple experiment, that succeeds in many cases even with unpractised persons, will serve to illustrate this. The experimenter thinks, say, of the number *four*, and then waits, his hands quietly resting on the table, until he feels that the table makes the first inclination to announce the number thought of. He lifts his hands off the table immediately, and the number *four* will be correctly tilted out. It is advisable in this experiment to place the table upon a soft thick carpet. By close attention the experimenter

---

hand drew small, more or less faithful, copies of figures which were vividly presented. These purposeful tremors can be demonstrated in a very simple way by experiments with the pendulum.

will occasionally notice a movement of the table which is thus represented (*See Fig 2*).

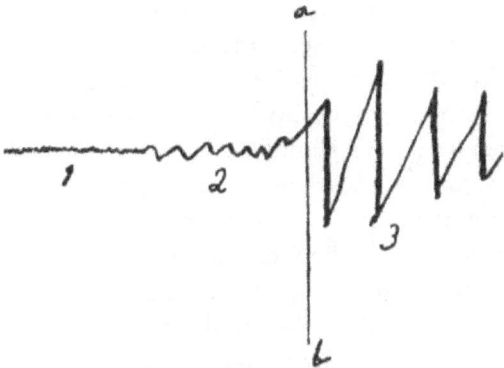

FIG. 2.

(1) Purposeful tremors too slight to be perceived by the subject.

(2) Several very small but perceptible oscillations of the table which indicate that the subject is responding to them.

(3) The big movements (tilts) of the table, giving the number four that was thought of.

(*ab*) Denotes the moment when the operator's hands are removed.

This experiment succeeds excellently with well-disposed but inexperienced subjects. After a little practice the phenomenon indicated is wont to disappear, since by practice the number is read and reproduced directly from the purposeful movements.[*]

In a responsive medium these purposeful tremors of the experimenter act just as the intentional taps in the experiment cited above; they are received, strengthened and reproduced, although slightly wavering. Still they are perceptible and hence act suggestively as slight tactile stimuli, and by the increase of partial hypnosis give rise to great automatic movements. This experiment illustrates in the clearest way the increase step by step of autosuggestion. Along the path of this auto-suggestion are developed all the automatic phenomena of a motor nature. How the intellectual content gradually mingles in with the purely motor need scarcely be elucidated after this discussion. There is no need of a special suggestion for the evoking of intellectual phenomena. From the outset it is a question of word-presentation, at least from the side of the experimenter. After the first aimless motor irrelevancies of the unpractised subject, some word-products or the intentions of the experimenter are soon reproduced. Objectively the occurrence of an intellectual content must be understood as follows: —

---

[*] Cf. Preyer, "Die Erklärung des Gedankenlesens," Leipzig, 1886.

By the gradual increase of auto-suggestion the motor-range of the arm becomes isolated from consciousness, that is to say, the perception of the slight movement-impulse is concealed from consciousness.[°]

By the knowledge gained from consciousness that some intellectual content is possible, there results a collateral excitation in the speech-area as the means immediately at hand for intellectual notification. The motor part of word-presentation is necessarily chiefly concerned with this aiming at notification.[†] In this way we understand the unconscious flowing over of speech-impulse to the motor-area[‡] and conversely the gradual penetration of partial hypnosis into the speech-area.

In numerous experiments with beginners, as a rule I have observed at the beginning of intellectual phenomena a relatively large

---

[°] Analogous to certain hypnotic experiments in the waking state. Cf. Janet's experiment when by a whispered suggestion he induced a patient to lie flat on the ground without being aware of it ("L'Automatisme").

[†] Charcot's scheme of word-picture combination: 1, Auditory image. 2, Visual image. 3, Motor image., Speech image., Writing image. In Gilbert Ballet, "Die innerliche Sprache," Leipzig and Wien, 1890.

[‡] Bain says, "Thought is a suppressed word or a suppressed act" ("The Senses and the Intellect").

number of completely meaningless words, also often a series of meaningless single letters. Later on, all kinds of absurdities are produced, *e.g.* words or entire sentences with the letters irregularly misplaced or with the order of the letters all reversed—a kind of mirror-writing. The appearance of the letter or word indicates a new suggestion; some sort of association is involuntarily joined to it, which is then realised. Remarkably enough, these are not generally the conscious associations, but quite unexpected ones, a circumstance showing that a considerable part of the speech-area is already hypnotically isolated. The recognition of this automatism again forms a fruitful suggestion, since invariably at this moment the feeling of strangeness arises, if it is not already present in the pure motor-automatism. The question, "Who is doing this?" "Who is speaking?", is the suggestion for the synthesis of the unconscious personality which as a rule does not like being kept waiting too long. Any name is introduced, generally one charged with emotion, and the automatic splitting of the personality is accomplished. How accidental and how vacillating this synthesis is at its beginning, the following reports from the literature show. Myers[*] communicates the following interesting observation on a Mr. A.,

---

[*] *Proceedings of S.P.R.*, 1885. "Automatic writing."

a member of the Society for Psychical Research, who was making experiments on himself in automatic writing.

THIRD DAY.

Question: What is man?

Answer: *TEFI H HASL ESBLE LIES*.

Is that an anagram? *Yes*.

How many words does it contain? *Five*.

What is the first word? *SEE*.

What is the second word? *SEEEE*.

See? Shall I interpret it myself? *Try to*.

Mr. A. found this solution: "Life is less able." He was astonished at this intellectual information, which seemed to him to prove the existence of an intelligence independent of his own. Therefore he went on to ask:

Who are you? *Clelia*.

Are you a woman? *Yes*.

Have you ever lived upon the earth? *No*.

Will you come to life? *Yes*.

When? *In six years*.

Why are you conversing with me? *E if Clelia el*.

Mr. A. interpreted this answer as: *I Clelia feel*.

FOURTH DAY.

Question: Am I the one who asks the questions? *Yes*.

Is Clelia there? *No*.

Who is here then? *Nobody*.

Does Clelia exist at all? *No*.

With whom then was I speaking yesterday? *With no one.*

From these quotations it will be seen in what way the subconscious personality is constructed. It owes its origin purely to suggestive questions meeting a certain disposition of the medium. The explanation is the result of the disintegration of the psychical complex; the feeling of the strangeness of such automatisms then comes in to help, as soon as conscious attention is directed to the automatic act. The individualisation of the subconsciousness always denotes a considerable further step of great suggestive influence upon the further formation of automatisms.° So, too, we must regard the origin of the unconscious personalities in our case.

The objection that there is simulation in automatic table-turning may well be given up, when one considers the phenomenon of thought-reading from the purposeful tremors which the patient offered in such plenitude. Rapid, conscious thought-reading demands at the least an extraordinary degree of practice, which it has been shown the patient did not possess. By means of the purposeful tremors whole conversations can be carried on, as in

---

° "*Une fois baptisé, le personnage inconscient est plus déterminé et plus net, il montre mieux ses caractères psychologiques*" (Janet, "L'Automatisme," p. 318).

our case. In the same way the suggestibility of the subconscious can be proved objectively if, for instance, the experimenter with his hand on the table desires that the hand of the medium should no longer be able to move the table or the glass; contrary to all expectation and to the liveliest astonishment of the subject, the table will immediately remain immovable. Naturally any other desired suggestions can be realised, provided they do not overstep by their innervations the region of partial hypnosis; this proves at the same time the limited nature of the hypnosis. Suggestions for the legs and the other arm will thus not be obeyed. Table-turning was not an automatism which belonged exclusively to the patient's semi-somnambulism: on the contrary, it occurred in the most pronounced form in the waking state, and in most cases then passed over into semi-somnambulism, the appearance of this being generally announced by hallucinations, as it was at the first sitting.

2. *Automatic writing.* — A second automatic phenomenon, which at the outset corresponds to a higher degree of partial hypnosis, is automatic writing. It is, according to my experience, much rarer and more difficult to produce than table-turning. As in table-turning, it is again a matter of a primary suggestion, to the conscious when sensibility is retained, to the unconscious when it is obliterated. The

suggestion is, however, not a simple one, for it already bears in itself an intellectual element. "To write" means "to write something." This special element of the suggestion, which extends beyond the merely motor, often conditions a certain perplexity on the part of the subject, giving rise to slight contrary suggestions which hinder the appearance of the automatisms. I have observed in a few cases that the suggestion is realised, despite its relative venturesomeness (*e.g.* one directed towards the waking consciousness of a so-called normal person). However, it takes place in a peculiar way; it first displaces the purely motor part of the central system concerned in hypnosis, and the deeper hypnosis is then reached by auto-suggestion from the motor phenomenon, analogous to the procedure in table-turning described above. The subject,[*] who has a pencil in his hand, is purposely engaged in conversation whilst his attention is diverted from the writing. The hand begins to make movements, beginning with many upward strokes and zigzag lines, or a simple line is made. Occasionally it happens that the pencil does not touch the paper, but writes in the air. These movements must be conceived as purely motor phenomena, which correspond

---

[*] Cf. the corresponding experiments of Binet and Féré. See Binet, "Les Altérations."

to the expression of the motor element in the presentation "write." This phenomenon is somewhat rare; generally single letters are first written, and what was said above of table-turning holds true of their combination into words and sentences. True mirror-writing is also observed here and there. In the majority of cases, and perhaps in all experiments with beginners who are not under some very special suggestion, the automatic writing is that of the subject. Occasionally its character may be greatly changed,° but this is secondary, and is always to be regarded as a symptom of the intruding synthesis of a subconscious personality.

FIG. 3.

As stated, the patient's automatic writing never came to any very great development. In these experiments, generally carried out in

---

° Cf. Corresponding tests by Flournoy: "Des Indes à la planète Mara. Etude sur un cas de somnambulisme avec glossolalie." Paris and Genève, 1900.

darkness, she passed over into semi-somnambulism, or into ecstasy. The automatic writing had thus the same effect as the preliminary table-turning.

3. *The Hallucinations* — The nature of the passing into somnambulism in the second séance is of psychological importance. As stated, the automatic phenomena were progressing favourably when darkness came on. The most interesting event of this séance, so far, was the brusque interruption of the communication from the grandfather, which was the starting-point of various debates amongst the members of the circle. These two momentous occurrences, the darkness and the striking event, seem to have been the foundation for a rapid deepening of hypnosis, in consequence of which the hallucinations could be developed. The psychological mechanism of this process seems to be as follows. The influence of darkness upon the suggestibility of the sense-organs is well known.[*] Binet[†] states that it has a special influence on hysterics, producing a state of sleepiness. As is clear from the foregoing, the patient was in a state of partial hypnosis and had constituted herself one with the unconscious personality in

---

[*] Cf. Hagen, "Zur Theorie des Hallucinationen," *Allg. Zeitschrift f. Psych.*, XXV. 10.
[†] Binet, "Les Altérations," p. 157.

closest relationship to her in the domain of speech. The automatic expression of this personality is interrupted most unexpectedly by a new person, of whose existence no one had any suspicion. Whence came this cleavage? Obviously the eager expectation of this first séance had very much occupied the patient. Her reminiscences of me and my family had probably grouped themselves around this expectation; hence these suddenly come to light at the climax of the automatic expression. That it was just my grandfather and no one else — not, *e.g.*, my deceased father, who, as she knew, was much closer to me than the grandfather whom I had never known — perhaps suggests where the origin of this new person is to be sought. It is probably a dissociation of the personality already present which seized upon the material next at hand for its expression, namely, upon the associations concerning myself. How far this is parallel to the experiences revealed by dream investigation (Freud's°) must remain undecided, for we have no means of judging how far the effect mentioned can be considered a "repressed" one. From the brusque interruption of the new personality, we may conclude

---

° "Die Traumdeutung," 1900. ["The Interpretation of Dreams," translated by Dr. A. A. Brill. London: Allen & Unwin, 1918.]

that the presentations concerned were very vivid, with corresponding intensity of expectation. This perhaps was an attempt to overcome a certain maidenly shyness and embarrassment. This event reminds us vividly of the manner in which the dream presents to consciousness, by a more or less transparent symbolism, things one has never said to oneself clearly and openly. We do not know when this dissociation of the new personality occurred, whether it had been slowly prepared in the unconscious, or whether it first occurred in the séance. In any case, this event meant a considerable increase in the extension of the unconscious sphere rendered accessible through the hypnosis. At the same time this event must be regarded as powerfully suggestive in regard to the impression which it made upon the waking consciousness of the patient. For the perception of this unexpected intervention of a new power must inevitably excite a feeling of the strangeness of the automatisms, and would easily suggest the thought that an independent spirit is here making itself known. Hence the intelligible association that she would finally be able to see this spirit. The situation that ensued at the second séance is to be explained by the coincidence of this energising suggestion with the heightened suggestibility conditioned by the darkness. The hypnosis, and with it the series of dissociated presentations, break through to the visual area, and the expression of the unconscious, hitherto purely motor, is made objective, according to the measure of the specific energy of the new system, in the shape of visual images with the character of hallucinations; not as a mere accompanying phenomenon of the word-automatism, but as a substituted function. The explanation of the situation that arose in the first séance, at that time unexpected and inexplicable, is no longer presented in words, but as a descriptive allegorical vision. The sentence "they do not hate one another, but are friends," is expressed in a picture. We often encounter events of this kind in somnambulism. The thinking of somnambulists is given in plastic images which constantly break into this or that sense-sphere and are made objective in hallucinations. The process of reflection sinks into the subconscious; only its end-results arise to consciousness either as presentations vividly tinged by the senses, or directly as hallucinations. In our case the same thing occurred as in the patient whose anæsthetic hand Binet pricked nine times, making her think of the figure 9; or as in Flournoy's[°] Helen Smith, who, when asked during business-hours about certain patterns, suddenly saw the number of days (18) for

---

[°] Flournoy, *l.c.*, p. 55.

which they had been lent, at a length of 20 mm. in front of her. The further question arises, why does the automatism appear in the visual and not in the acoustic sphere? There are several grounds for this choice of the visual sphere.

(1) The patient is not gifted acoustically; she is, for instance, very unmusical.

(2) There was no stillness corresponding to the darkness which might have favoured the appearance of sounds; there was a lively conversation.

(3) The increased conviction of the near presence of spirits, because the automatism felt so strange, could easily have aroused the idea that a spirit might be seen, thus causing a slight excitation of the visual sphere.

(4) The entoptic phenomena in darkness favoured the occurrence of hallucinations.

The reasons (3) and (4) — the entoptic phenomena in the darkness and the probable excitation of the visual sphere — are of decisive importance for the appearance of hallucinations. The entoptic phenomena in this case play the same role in the auto-suggestion, the production of the automatism, as the slight tactile stimuli in hypnosis of the motor centre. As stated, flashes preceded the first hallucinatory twilight-state. Obviously attention was already at a high pitch, and directed to visual perceptions, so that the retina's own light, usually very weak, was seen with great intensity. The part played by entoptic perceptions of light in the origin of hallucinations deserves further consideration. Schüle[°] says: "The swarming of light and colour which stimulates and animates the field of vision, although in the dark, supplies the material for phantastic figures in the air before falling asleep. As we know, absolute darkness is never seen; a few particles of the dark field of vision are always illumined; flecks of light move here and there, and combine into all kinds of figures; it only needs a moderately active imagination to create out of them, as one does out of clouds, certain known figures. The power of reasoning, fading as one falls asleep, leaves phantasy free play to construct very vivid figures. In the place of the light spots, haziness and changing colours of the dark visual field, there arise definite outlines of objects."[†]

In this way hypnagogic hallucinations arise. The chief *rôle* naturally belongs to the imagination, hence imaginative people in particular are subject to hypnagogic hallucinations.[‡] The hypnopompic hallucinations described by Myers arise in the same way.

[°] Schüle, "Handbuch," p. 134.

[†] J. Müller, quoted *Allg. Zeit. f. Psych.*, XXV. 41.

[‡] Spinoza hypnopompically saw a *"nigrum et scabiosum Brasilianum."* —J. Müller, *l.c.* In Goethe's

It is highly probable that hypnagogic pictures are identical with the dream-pictures of normal sleep—forming their visual foundation. Maury[°] has proved from self-observation that the pictures which hovered around him hypnagogically were also the objects of the dreams that followed. G. Trumbull Ladd[†] has shown this even more convincingly. By practice he succeeded in waking himself suddenly two to five minutes after falling asleep. He then observed that the figures dancing before the retina at times represented the same contours as the pictures just dreamed of. He even states that nearly every visual dream is shaped by the retina's own light-figures. In our case the fantastic rendering of these pictures was favoured by the situation. We must not underrate the influence of the over-excited expectation which allowed

---

"The Elective Affinities," at times in the half darkness Ottilie saw the figure of Edward in a dimly-lit spot. Compare also Cardanus, *"imagines videbam ab imo lecti, quasi e parvulis annulis arcisque constantes, arborum, belluarum, hominum, oppidorum, instructarum acierum, bellicorum et musicorum instrumentorum aliorumque huius generis adscendentes, vicissimque descendentes, aliis atque aliis succedentibus"* (Hieronymus Cardanus, *"De subtilitate rerum"*).

[°] "Le sommeil et les rêves," p. 134.

[†] G. Trumbull Ladd, "Contribution to the Psychology of Visual Dreams," *Mind*, April, 1892.

the dull retina-light to appear with increased intensity.* The further formation of the retinal appearances follows in accordance with the predominating presentations. That hallucinations appear in this way has been also observed in other visionaries. Jeanne d'Arc first saw a cloud of light, and only after some time there stepped forth St. Michael, St. Catherine and St. Margaret. For a whole hour Swedenborg† saw nothing but illuminated spheres and fiery flames. He felt a mighty change in the brain, which seemed to him "release of light." After the space of one hour he suddenly saw red figures which he regarded as angels and spirits. The sun visions of Benvenuto Cellini‡ in Engelsburg are probably of the same nature. A student who frequently saw apparitions stated: "When these apparitions come, at first I only see single masses of light and at the same time am conscious of a dull noise in the ears. Gradually these contours become clear figures."

---

* Hecker says of the same condition, "There is a simple elemental vision, even without sense presentation, through over-excitation of mental activity, not leading to phantastic imagery, that is the vision of light free from form, a manifestation of the visual organs stimulated from within" ("Ueber Visionen," Berlin, 1848).

† Hagen, l.c., p. 57.

‡ Goethe, "Benvenuto Cellini."

At all times the complex hallucinations of visionaries have occupied a peculiar place in scientific criticism. Macario[°] early separated these so-called intuition-hallucinations from others, since he maintains that they occur in persons of an eager mind, deep understanding and high nervous excitability. Hecker expresses himself similarly but more enthusiastically.

His view is that their condition is "the congenital high development of the spiritual organ which calls into active, free and mobile play the life of the imagination, bringing it spontaneous activity."[†] These hallucinations are "precursors or signs of mighty spiritual power." The vision is "an increased excitation which is harmoniously adapted to the most complete health of mind and body." The complex hallucinations do not belong to the waking state, but prefer as a rule a partial waking state. The visionary is buried in his vision even to complete annihilation. Flournoy was also always able to prove in the visions of H.S. *"un certain degré d'obnubilation."* In our case the vision is complicated by a state of sleep whose peculiarities we shall review later.

[°] *Allg. Zeit. f. Psych.*, IV. 139.
[†] *Ibid.*, VI. 285.

V

THE CHANGE IN CHARACTER

THE most striking characteristic of the second stage in our case is the change in character. We meet many cases in the literature which have offered the symptom of spontaneous character-change. The first case in a scientific publication is Weir-Mitchell's[*] case of Mary Reynolds.

This was the case of a young woman living in Pennsylvania in 1811. After a deep sleep of about twenty hours she had totally forgotten her entire past and everything she had learnt; even the words she spoke had lost their meaning. She no longer knew her relatives. Slowly she re-learnt to read and write, but her writing was from right to left. More striking still was the change in her character. Instead of being melancholy, she was now cheerful in the extreme. Instead of being reserved, she was buoyant and sociable. Formerly taciturn and retiring, she was now merry and jocose. Her disposition was totally changed.

---

[*] Coll. Physicians of Philadelphia, April 4, 1888. Also *Harper's Magazine*, 1869. Abstracted in extenso in William James's "Principles of Psychology," 1891, p. 391 ff.

In this state she renounced her former retired life and liked to undertake adventurous excursions unarmed, through wood and mountain, on foot and horseback. In one of these excursions she encountered a large black bear, which she took for a pig. The bear raised himself on his hind legs and gnashed his teeth at her. As she could not drive her horse on any further, she took an ordinary stick and hit the bear until it took to flight. Five weeks later, after a deep sleep, she returned to her earlier state with amnesia for the interval. These states alternated for about sixteen years. But her last twenty-five years Mary Reynolds passed exclusively in her second state.[*]

Schroeder von der Kalk[†] reports on the following case: The patient became ill at the age of sixteen with periodic amnesia, after a previous tedious illness of three years. Sometimes in the morning after waking she passed through a peculiar choreic state, during which she made rhythmical movements with her arms. Throughout the whole day she would then exhibit a childish, silly behaviour and lost

---

[*] Cf. Emminghaus, "Allg. Psychopathologie," p. 129, Ogier Ward's case.

[†] Schroeder von der Kalk, "Pathologie und Therapie der Geisteskrankheiten," p. 31: Braunschweig, 1863. Quoted in *Allg. Zeit. f. Psych.*, XXII., p. 405.

all her educated capabilities. (When normal she is very intelligent, well-read, speaks French well.) In the second state she begins to speak faulty French. On the second day she is again at times normal. The two states are completely separated by amnesia.[°]

Hoefelt[†] reports on a case of spontaneous somnambulism in a girl who, in her normal state, was submissive and modest, but in somnambulism was impertinent, rude and violent. Azam's[‡] Felida was, in her normal state, depressed, inhibited, timid; and in the second state lively, confident, enterprising to recklessness. The second state gradually became the chief one, and finally so far suppressed the first state that the patient called her normal states, lasting now but a short time, "crises." The amnesic attacks had begun at 14½. In time the second state became milder and there was a certain approximation between the character of the two states. A very striking example of change in character is that worked out by Camuset, Ribot, Legrand du Saulle, Richer, Voisin, and put together by Bourru

---

[°] Cf. Donath, "Ueber Suggestibilität," Wiener mediz. Presse, 1832, No. 31. Quoted *Arch. f. Psych.*, XXXII., p. 335.

[†] Hoefelt. *Allg. Zeit. f. Psych.*, XLIX., p. 200.

[‡] Azam, "Hypnotisme, Double Conscience," etc.

and Burot.[°] It is that of Louis V., a severe male hysteric with amnesic alternating character. In the first stage he is rude, cheeky, querulous, greedy, thievish, inconsiderate. In the second state he is an agreeable, sympathetic character, industrious, docile and obedient. This amnesic change of character has been used by Paul Lindau[†] in his drama "Der Andere" (The Other One).

Rieger[‡] reports on a case parallel to Lindau's criminal lawyer. The unconscious personalities of Janet's Lucie and Léonie (Janet, *l.c.*) and Morton Prince's[§] may also be regarded as parallel with our case. There are, however, therapeutic artificial products whose importance lies in the domain of the dissociation of consciousness and of memory.

In the above cases, the second state is always separated from the first by an amnesic dissociation, and the change in character is, at times, accompanied by a break in the continuity of consciousness. In our case there is no amnesic disturbance; the passage from the first to the second stage follows quite

---

[°] Bourru et Burot, "Changements de Personnnalité," 1888.

[†] Moll, "Zeit. f. Hypn.," I., 306.

[‡] Rieger, "Der Hypnotismus," 1884, p. 190 ff.

[§] Morton Prince, "An Experimental Study of Visions," Brain, 1898.

gradually and the continuity of consciousness remains. The patient carries out in her waking state everything, otherwise unknown to her, from the field of the unconscious that she has experienced during hallucinations in the second stage.

Periodic changes in personality without amnesic dissociation are found in the region of *folie circulaire*, but are rarely seen in hysterics, as Renaudin's[*] case shows. A young man, whose behaviour had always been excellent, suddenly began to display the worst tendencies. There were no symptoms of insanity, but, on the other hand, the whole surface of the body was anæsthetic. This state showed periodic intervals, and in the same way the patient's character was subject to vacillations. As soon as the anæsthesia disappeared he was manageable and friendly. When the anæsthesia returned he was overcome by the worst instincts, which, it was observed, even included the wish to murder.

Remembering that our patient's age at the beginning of the disturbances was 14-1/2, that is, the age of puberty had just been reached, one must suppose that there was some connection between the disturbances and the physiological character-changes at puberty. "There appears in the consciousness of the

---

[*] Quoted by Ribot, "Die Persönlichkeit."

individual during this period of life a new group of sensations, together with the feelings and ideas arising therefrom; this continuous pressure of unaccustomed mental states makes itself constantly felt because the cause is always at work; the states are co-ordinated because they arise from one and the same source, and must little by little bring about deep-seated changes in the ego."[°] Vacillating moods are easily recognisable; the confused new, strong feelings, the inclination towards idealism, to exalted religiosity and mysticism, side by side with the falling back into childishness, all this gives to adolescence its prevailing character. At this epoch the human being first makes clumsy attempts at independence in every direction; for the first time uses for his own purposes all that family and school have contributed hitherto; he conceives ideals, constructs far-reaching plans for the future, lives in dreams whose content is ambitious and egotistic. This is all physiological. The puberty of a psychopathic is a crisis of more serious import. Not only do the psychophysical changes run a stormy course, but features of a hereditary degenerate character become fixed. In the child these do not appear at all, or but sporadically. For the explanation of our case we are bound to consider a specific

---

[°] *Ibid.*, p. 69.

disturbance of puberty. The reasons for this view will appear from a further study of the second personality. (For the sake of brevity we shall call the second personality IVENES — as the patient baptised her higher ego).

Ivenes is the exact continuation of the everyday ego. She includes the whole of her conscious content. In the semi-somnambulic state her intercourse with the real external world is analogous to that of the waking state, that is, she is influenced by recurrent hallucinations, but no more than persons who are subject to non-confusional psychotic hallucinations. The continuity of Ivenes obviously extends to the hysterical attack with its dramatic scenes, visionary events, etc. During the attack itself she is generally isolated from the external world; she does not notice what is going on around her, does not know that she is talking loudly, etc. But she has no amnesia for the dream-content of her attack. Amnesia for her motor expressions and for the changes in her surroundings is not always present. That this is dependent upon the degree of intensity of her somnambulic state and that there is sometimes partial paralysis of individual sense organs is proved by the occasion when she did not notice me; her eyes were then open, and most probably she saw the others, although she only perceived me when I spoke to her. This is a case of so-called *systematised anæsthesia* (negative hallucination) which is often observed in hysterics.

Flournoy,[*] for instance, reports of Helen Smith that during the séances she suddenly ceased to see those taking part, although she still heard their voices and felt their touch; sometimes she no longer heard, although she saw the movements of the lips of the speakers, etc.

Ivenes is just the continuation of the waking self. She contains the entire consciousness of S. W.'s waking state. Her remarkable behaviour tells decidedly against any analogy with cases of *double consciousness*. The characteristics of Ivenes contrast favourably with the patient's ordinary self. She is a calmer, more composed personality; her pleasing modesty and accuracy, her uniform intelligence, her confident way of talking must be regarded as an improvement of the whole being; thus far there is analogy with Janet's Léonie. But this is the extent of the similarity. Apart from the amnesia, they are divided by a deep psychological difference. Léonie II. is the healthier, the more normal; she has regained her natural capabilities, she shows remarkable improvement upon her chronic condition of hysteria. Ivenes rather gives the impression of a more artificial product; there is

---

[*] Flournoy, *l.c.*, p. 59.

something thought out; despite all her excellences she gives the impression of playing a part excellently; her world-sorrow, her yearning for the other side of things, are not merely piety but the attributes of saintliness. Ivenes is no mere human, but a mystic being who only partly belongs to reality. The mournful features, the attachment to sorrow, her mysterious fate, lead us to the historic prototype of Ivenes—Justinus Kerner's "Prophetess of Prevorst." Kerner's book must be taken as known, and therefore I omit any references to these common traits. But Ivenes is no copy of the prophetess; she lacks the resignation and the saintly piety of the latter. The prophetess is merely used by her as a study for her own original conception. The patient pours her own soul into the *rôle* of the prophetess, thus seeking to create an ideal of virtue and perfection. She anticipates her future. She incarnates in Ivenes what she wishes to be in twenty years—the assured, influential, wise, gracious, pious lady. It is in the construction of the second person that there lies the far-reaching difference between Léonie II. and Ivenes. Both are psychogenic. But Léonie I. receives in Léonie II. what really belongs to her, while S. W. builds up a person beyond herself. It cannot be said "she deceives

herself" into, but that "she dreams herself"
into the higher ideal state.°

The realisation of this dream recalls vividly
the psychology of the pathological cheat. Delbruck[†] and Forel[‡] have indicated the importance of auto-suggestion in the formation
of pathological cheating and reverie. Pick[§] re-
gards intense auto-suggestibility as the first
symptom of the hysterical dreamer, making
possible the realisation of the "day-dream."
One of Pick's patients dreamt that she was in
a morally dangerous situation, and finally carried out an attempt at rape on herself; she lay
on the floor naked and fastened herself to a

° "Les rêves somnambuliques, sortes de romans
de l'imagination subliminale, analogues à ces his-
toires continues, que tant de gens se racontent à
eux-mêmes et dont ils sont généralement les hé-
ros dans leurs moments de far niente ou d'occu-
pations routinières qui n'offrent qu'un faible ob-
stacle aux rêveries intérieures. Constructions fan-
taisistes, millefois reprises et poursuivies, rare-
ment achevées, où la folle du logis se donne libre
carrière et prend sa revanche du terne et plat
terre à terre des réalités quotidiennes."
(Flournoy, *l.c.*, p. 8).
[†] Delbruck, "Die Pathologische Lüge."
[‡] Forel, "Hypnotisme."
[§] Pick, "Ueber Path. Träumerei und ihre Bezi-
ehung zur Hysterie," *Jahr. f. Psych. und Neur.*,
XIV., p. 280.

table and chairs. Or some dramatic person will be created with whom the patient enters into correspondence by letter, as in Bohn's case.[*] The patient dreamt herself into an engagement with a totally imaginary lawyer in Nice, from whom she received letters which she had herself written in disguised handwriting. This pathological dreaming, with autosuggestive deceptions of memory amounting to real delusions and hallucinations, is preeminently to be found in the lives of many saints.[†]

It is only a step from the dreamlike images strongly stamped by the senses to the true complex hallucinations.[‡] In Pick's case, for instance, one sees that the patient, who persuades herself that she is the Empress Elizabeth, gradually loses herself in her dreams to such an extent that her condition must be regarded as a true "twilight" state. Later it passes over into hysterical delirium, when her dream-phantasies become typical hallucinations. The pathological liar, who becomes involved through his phantasies, behaves exactly like a child who loses himself in his play,

---

[*] Bohn, "Ein Fall von doppelten Bewusstsein Diss." Breslau, 1898.

[†] Görres, l.c.

[‡] Cf. Behr, *Allg. Zeit. f. Psych.*, LVI., 918, and Ballet, *l.c.*, p. 44.

or like the actor who loses himself in his part.° There is here no fundamental distinction from somnambulic dissociation of personality, but only a difference of degree, which rests upon the intensity of the primary auto-suggestibility or disintegration of the psychic elements. *The more consciousness becomes dissociated, the greater becomes the plasticity of the dream situation, the less becomes the amount of conscious lying and of consciousness in general.* This being carried away by interest in the object is what Freud calls *hysterical.* For instance, to Erler's† acutely hysterical patient there appeared hypnagogically little riders made of paper, who so took possession of her imagination that she had the feeling of being herself one of them. Similar phenomena normally occur to us in dreams in general, in which we think like "hysterics."‡

The complete abandonment to the interesting image explains also the wonderful naturalness of pseudological or somnambulic

---

° Cf. *Redlich, Allg. Zeit. f. Psych.,* LVII., 66.
† Erler, *Allg. Zeit. f. Psych.,* XXXV., 21.
‡ Binet, "Les hystériques ne sont pas pour nous que des sujets d'élection agrandissant des phénomènes qu'on doit nécessairement retrouver à quelque degré chez une foule d'autres personnes qui ne sont ni atteintes ni même effleurées par la névrose hystérique". ("Les altérations," p. 29)

representation — a degree unattainable in conscious acting. The less waking consciousness intervenes by reflection and reasoning, the more certain and convincing becomes the objectivation of the dream, e.g. the roof-climbing of somnambulists.

Our case has another analogy with pseudologia phantastica: the development of the phantasies during the attacks. Many cases are known in the literature where the pathological lying comes on in attacks and during serious hysterical trouble.[*]

Our patient develops her systems exclusively in the attack. In her normal state she is quite incapable of giving any new ideas or explanations; she must either transpose herself into somnambulism or await its spontaneous appearance. This exhausts the affinity to *pseudologia phantastica* and to pathological dream-states.

Our patient's state is even differentiated from pathological dreaming, since it could never be proved that her dream-weavings had at any time previously been the objects of her interest during the day. Her dreams occur explosively, break forth with bewildering

---

[*] Delbrück, *l.c.*, and Redlich, *l.c.* Cf. the development of delusions in epileptic stupor mentioned by Mörchen, "Essay on Stupor," pp. 51 and 59, 1901.

completeness from the darkness of the unconscious. Exactly the same was the case in
Flournoy's Helen Smith. In many cases (see
below), however, links with the perceptions
of the normal states can be demonstrated: it
seems therefore probable that the roots of
every dream were originally images with an
emotional accentuation, which, however, only
occupied waking consciousness for a short
time.° We must allow that in the origin of such
dreams hysterical forgetfulness† plays a part
not to be underestimated.

° Cf. Flournoy's very interesting supposition as to
the origin of the Hindu *cycle* of H.S.: "Je ne serais
pas étonné que la remarque de Martes sur la
beauté des femmes du Kanara ait été le clou,
l'atome crochu, qui a piqué l'attention subliminale et l'a très naturellement rivée sur cette
unique passage avec les deux ou trois lignes
consécutives, à l'exclusion de tout le contexte en-
vironnant beaucoup moins intérressant" (*L.c.*, p.
285).
† Janet says, "From forgetfulness there arises frequently, even if not invariably, the so-called lying
of hysteria. The same explanation holds good of a
hysteric's whims, changes of mood, ingratitude—
in a word, of his inconstancy. The link between
the past and present, which gives to the whole
personality its seriousness and poise, depends to
a large extent upon memory" ("Mental States,"
etc., p. 67).

Many images are buried which would be sufficient to put the consciousness on guard; associated classes of ideas are lost and go on spinning their web in the unconscious, thanks to the psychic dissociation; this is a process which we meet again in the genesis of our dreams.

"Our conscious reflection teaches us that when exercising attention we pursue a definite course. But if that course leads us to an idea which does not meet with our approval, we discontinue and cease to apply our attention. Now, apparently, the chain of thought thus started and abandoned, may go on without regaining attention unless it reaches a spot of especially marked intensity, which compels renewed attention. An initial rejection, perhaps consciously brought about by the judgment on the ground of incorrectness or unfitness for the actual purpose of the mental act, may therefore account for the fact that a mental process continues unnoticed by consciousness until the onset of sleep."[*]

In this way we may explain the apparently sudden and direct appearance of dream-states. The entire carrying over of the conscious personality into the dream-role involves indirectly the development of simultaneous automatisms.

---

[*] Freud, "The Interpretation of Dreams," p. 469.

Our subject's romances throw a most significant light on the subjective roots of her dreams. They swarm with secret and open love-affairs, with illegitimate births and other sexual insinuations. The central point of all these ambiguous stories is a lady whom she dislikes, who is gradually made to assume the form of her polar opposite, and whilst Ivenes becomes the pinnacle of virtue, this lady is a sink of iniquity. *But her reincarnation doctrines, in which she appears as the mother of countless thousands, arises in its naïve nakedness from an exuberant phantasy which is, of course, very characteristic of the period of puberty. It is the woman's premonition of the sexual feeling, the dream of fruitfulness, which the patient has turned into these monstrous ideas.* We shall not go wrong if we seek for the curious form of the disease in the teeming sexuality of this too-rich soil. Viewed from this standpoint, the whole creation of Ivenes, with her enormous family, is nothing but a dream of sexual wish-fulfilment, differentiated from the dream of a night only in that it persists for months and years.

VI

RELATION TO THE
HYSTERICAL ATTACK

SO far one point in S. W.'s history has remained unexplained, and that is her attack. In
the second séance she was suddenly seized
with a sort of fainting fit, from which she
awoke with a recollection of various hallucinations. According to her own statement, she
had not lost consciousness for a moment.
Judging from the external symptoms and the
course of the attack, one is inclined to regard
it as a *narcolepsy*, or rather a *lethargy*; such, for
example, as Loewenfeld has described, and
the more readily as we know that previously
one member of her family (her grandmother)
has had an attack of lethargy. It is possible to
imagine that the *lethargic disposition* (Loewenfeld) had descended to our subject. In spiritualistic séances it is not usual to see hysterical
convulsions. Our subject showed no sort of
convulsive symptoms, but in their place, perhaps, the peculiar sleeping-states. Ætiologi-
cally, at the outset, two moments must be
taken into consideration:
  1. The irruption of hypnosis.
  2. The psychic stimulation.

1. *Irruption of partial hypnosis.* — Janet observes that the subconscious automatisms have a hypnotic influence and can bring about complete somnambulism.[*]

He made the following experiment: While the patient, who was in the completely waking state, was engaged in conversation by a second observer, Janet stationed himself behind her and by means of whispered suggestions made her unconsciously move her hand and by written signs give an answer to questions. Suddenly the patient broke off the conversation, turned round and with her supraliminal consciousness continued the previously subconscious talk with Janet. She had fallen into hypnotic somnambulism.[†]

There is here a state of affairs similar to our patient's. But it must be noted that, for certain reasons discussed later, the sleeping state is not to be regarded as hypnotic. We therefore come to the question of —

2. *The Psychic Stimulation.* — It is told of Bettina Brentano that the first time she met Goethe she suddenly fell asleep on his knee.[‡]

---

[*] "L'Automatisme," p. 329.

[†] Janet, *l.c.*, p. 329.

[‡] In literature Gustave Flaubert has made use of a similar falling asleep at the moment of extreme excitement in his novel "Salambo." When the hero, after many struggles, has at last captured

This ecstatic sleep in the midst of extremest torture, the so-called "witch-sleep," is well known in the history of trials for witchcraft.[*]

With susceptible subjects relatively insignificant stimuli suffice to bring about the somnambulic state. Thus a sensitive lady had to have a splinter cut out of her finger. Without any kind of bodily change she suddenly saw herself sitting by the side of a brook in a beautiful meadow, plucking flowers. This condition lasted as long as the slight operation and then disappeared spontaneously.[†]

Loewenfeld has noticed unintentional inducement of hysterical lethargy through hypnosis.[‡]

Our case has certain resemblances to hysterical lethargy[§] as described by Loewenfeld, viz. the shallow breathing, the diminution of the pulse, the corpse-like pallor of the face, and further the peculiar feeling of dying and the thoughts of death.[°°]

Salambo, he suddenly falls asleep just as he touches her virginal bosom.

[*] Perhaps the cases of paralysis of the emotions also belong here. Cf. Baetz, *Allg. Zeitsch. f. Psych.*, LVIII., p. 717.

[†] *Allg. Zeitsch. f. Psych.*, XXX., p. 17.

[‡] *Arch. f. Psych.*, XXIII., p. 59.

[§] Cf. here Flournoy, *l.c.*, 65.

[°°] *Arch. f. Psych.*, XXII., p. 737.

The retention of one sense is not incon-
sistent with lethargy: thus in certain cases of
trance the sense of hearing remains.[°]

In Bonamaison's[†] case not only was the
sense of touch retained, but the senses of hearing and smell were quickened. The hallucinatory content and loud speaking is also met
with in persons with hallucinations in lethargy.[‡] Usually there prevails total amnesia for
the lethargic interval. Loewenfeld's[§] case D.
had, however, a fleeting recollection; in
Bonamaison's case there was no amnesia. Lethargic patients do not prove susceptible to
the usual waking stimuli, but Loewenfeld succeeded with his patient St. in turning the lethargy into hypnosis by means of mesmeric
passes, thus combining it with the rest of consciousness during the attack.[°°] Our patient
showed herself absolutely insusceptible in the
beginning of the lethargy, but later on she began to speak spontaneously, was incapable of
giving any attention when her somnambulic
ego was speaking, but could attend when it

[°] *Ibid.*, 734.

[†] Bonamaison, "Un cas remarquable d'Hypnose
spontanée," etc. —*Rev. de l'Hypnotisme*, Fév. 1890,
p. 234.

[‡] *Arch. f. Psych.*, XXII., 737.

[§] *Ibid.*

[°°] *Ibid.*, XXIII., p. 59 ff.

was one of her automatic personalities. In this
last case it is probable that the hypnotic effect
of the automatisms succeeded in achieving a
partial transformation of the lethargy into
hypnosis. When we consider that, according
to Loewenfeld's view, the lethargic disposition must not be "too readily identified with
the peculiar condition of the nervous appa-
ratus in hysteria," then the idea of the family heredity of this disposition in our case becomes not a little probable. The disease is
much complicated by these attacks.

So far we have seen that the patient's consciousness of her ego is identical in all the
states. We have discussed two secondary
complexes of consciousness and have followed them into the somnambulic attack,
where they appear as the patient's vision
when she had lost her motor activity during
the attack. During the next attacks she was
impervious to any external incidents, but on
the other hand developed, within the twilight
state, all the more intense activity, in the form
of visions. It seems that many secondary series of ideas must have split off quite early
from the primary unconscious personality, for
already, after the first two séances, "spirits"
appeared by the dozen. The names were inex-
haustible in variety, but the differences between the personalities were soon exhausted
and it became apparent that they could all be

subsumed under two types, the *serious religious type* and the *gay-hilarious*. So far it was really only a matter of *two different unconscious personalities*, which appeared under different names but had no essential differences. The older type, the grandfather, who had initiated the automatisms, also first began to make use of the twilight state. I am not able to remember any suggestion which might have given rise to the automatic speaking. According to the preceding view, the attack in such circumstances might be regarded as a partial auto-hypnosis. The ego-consciousness which remains and, as a result of its isolation from the external world, occupies itself entirely with its hallucinations, is what is left over of the waking consciousness. Thus the automatism has a wide field for its activity. The independence of the individual central spheres which we have proved at the beginning to be present in the patient, makes the automatic act of speaking appear intelligible. Just as the dreamer on occasion speaks in his sleep, so, too, a man in his waking hours may accompany intensive thought with an unconscious whisper.° The peculiar movements of the speech-

---

° Cf. Lehman's investigations of involuntary whispering, "Aberglaube und Zauberei," 1898, p. 385 ff.

musculature are to be noted. They have also been observed in other somnambulists.[*]

These clumsy attempts must be directly paralleled with the unintelligent and clumsy movements of the table or glass, and most probably correspond to the *preliminary activity* of the motor portion of the presentation; that is to say, a stimulus limited to the motor-centre which has not previously been subordinated to any higher system. Whether the like occurs in persons who talk in their dreams, I do not know. But it has been observed in hypnotised persons.[†]

Since the convenient medium of speech was used as the means of communication, the study of the subconscious personalities was considerably lightened. Their intellectual compass is a relatively mediocre one. Their knowledge is greater than that of the waking patient, including also a few occasional details, such as the birthdays of dead strangers and the like. The source of these is more or

---

[*] Thus Flournoy writes, "Dans un premier essai Léopold (H.S.'s control-spirit) ne réussit qu'à donner ses intimations et sa pronunciation à Helen: après une séance où elle avait vivement souffert dans la bouche et le cou comme si on lui travaillait ou lui enlevait les organes vocaux, elle se mit à causer très naturellement."

[†] Loewenfeld, *Arch. f. Psych.*, XXIII., 60.

less obscure, since the patient does not know whence in the ordinary way she could have procured the knowledge of these facts. These are cases of so-called cryptomnesia, which are too unimportant to deserve more extended notice. The intelligence of the two subconscious persons is very slight; they produce banalities almost exclusively, but their relation to the conscious ego of the patient when in the somnambulic state is interesting. They are invariably aware of everything that takes place during ecstasy and occasionally they render an exact report from minute to minute.[*]

The subconscious persons only know the patient's phantastic changes of thought very superficially; they do not understand these and cannot answer a single question concerning the situation. Their stereotyped reference to Ivenes is: "Ask Ivenes." This observation reveals a dualism in the character of the subconscious personalities difficult to explain; for the grandfather, who gives information by automatic speech, also appears to Ivenes and, according to her account, teaches her about

---

[*] This behaviour recalls Flournoy's observations: "Whilst H.S. as a somnambule speaks as Marie Antoinette, the arms of H.S. do not belong to the somnambulic personality, but to the automatism Leopold, who converses by gestures with the observer" (Flournoy, *l.c.*, p. 125).

the objects in question. How is it that, when the grandfather speaks through the patient's mouth, he knows nothing of the very things which he himself teaches her in the ecstasies?

We must again return to the discussion of the first appearance of the hallucinations. We picture the vision, then, as an irruption of hypnosis into the visual sphere. That irruption does not lead to a "normal" hypnosis, but to a "hystero-hypnosis," that is, the simple hypnosis is complicated by a hysterical attack.

It is not a rare occurrence in the domain of hypnotism for normal hypnosis to be disturbed, or rather to be replaced by the unexpected appearance of hysterical somnambulism; the hypnotist in many cases then loses rapport with the patient. In our case the automatism arising in the motor area plays the part of hypnotist; the suggestions proceeding from it (called objective auto-suggestions) hypnotise the neighbouring areas in which a certain susceptibility has arisen. At the moment when the hypnotism flows over into the visual sphere, the hysterical attack occurs which, as remarked, effects a very deep-reaching change in a large portion of the psychical region. We must now suppose that the automatism stands in the same relationship to the attack as the hypnotist to a pathological hypnosis; its influence upon the further structure of the situation is lost. The hallucinatory appearance of the hypnotised personality, or rather of the suggested idea, may be regarded as the last effect upon the somnambulic personality. Thenceforward the hypnotist becomes only a figure with whom the somnambulic personality occupies itself independently: he can only state what is going on and is no longer the *conditio sine qua non* of the content of the somnambulic attack. The independent ego-complex of the attack, in our case Ivenes, has now the upper hand. She groups her own mental products around the personality of the hypnotiser, that is, of the grandfather, now degraded to a mere image. In this way we are enabled to understand the dualism in the character of the grandfather. *The grandfather I. who speaks directly to those present, is a totally different person and a mere spectator of his double, grandfather II., who appears as Ivenes' teacher.* Grandfather I. maintains energetically that both are one and the same person, and that I. has all the knowledge which II. possesses, and is only prevented from giving information by the difficulties of speech. (The dissociation was of course not realized by the patient, who took both to be one person.) Grandfather I., if closely examined, however, is not altogether wrong, judging from one fact which seems to make for the identity of I. and II., viz. that they are never both present together. When I. speaks automatically, II. is not present; Ivenes remarks on his absence. Similarly, during the ecstasy, when she is with II., she cannot say where I. is, or she may learn only on returning from an imaginary journey that meanwhile I. has been guarding her body. Conversely I. never says that he is going on a journey with Ivenes and never explains anything to her. This behaviour should be noted, for if I. is really separate from II., there seems no reason why he should not speak automatically at the same time that II. appears, and be present with II. in the ecstasy. Although this might have been supposed possible, as a matter of fact it was never observed. How is this dilemma to be resolved? At all events there exists an identity of I. and II., but it does not lie in the region of the personality under discussion; it lies in the basis common to both; that is, in the personality of the subject which in deepest essence is one and indivisible. Here we come across the characteristic of all hysterical dissociations of consciousness. *They are disturbances which only belong to the superficial, and none reaches so deep as to attack the strong-knit foundation of the ego-complex.*

In many such cases we can find the bridge which, although often well-concealed, spans the apparently impassable abyss. For instance, by suggestion, one of four cards is made invisible to a hypnotised person; he thereupon names the other three. A pencil is placed in his hand with the instruction to write down all the cards lying there; he correctly adds the fourth one.[°]

In the aura of his hystero-epileptic attacks a patient of Janet's[†] invariably had a vision of a conflagration, and whenever he saw an open fire he had an attack; indeed, the sight of a lighted match was sufficient to bring about an attack. The patient's visual field on the left side was limited to 30°, the right eye was shut. The left eye was fixed in the middle of a perimeter whilst a lighted match was held at 80°. The hystero-epileptic attack took place immediately. Despite the extensive amnesia in many cases of double consciousness, the patients' behaviour does not correspond to the degree of their ignorance, but it seems rather as if a deeper instinct guided their actions in accordance with their former knowledge. Not only this relatively slight amnesic dissociation, but the severe amnesia of the epileptic twilight-state, formerly regarded as *irreparabile damnum*, does not suffice to cut the inmost threads which bind the ego-complex in the twilight-state to the normal ego. In one case

---

[°] Dessoir, "Das Doppel-Ich," II. Aufl., 1896, p. 29.
[†] Janet, "L'anesthésie hystérique," *Arch. d'Neur.*, 69, 1892.

the content of the twilight-state could be grafted on to the waking ego-complex.[*]

Making use of these experiments for our case, we obtain the helpful hypothesis that those layers of the unconscious beyond reach of the dissociation endeavour to present the unity of automatic personality. This endeavour is shattered in the deeper-seated and more elemental disturbance of the hysterical attack,[†] which prevents a more complete synthesis by the tacking on of associations which are to a certain extent the most original individual property of supraliminal personality. As the Ivenes dream emerged it was fitted on to the figures accidentally in the field of vision, and henceforth remains associated with them.

---

[*] Graeter, *Zeit. f. Hypnotismus*, VIII., p. 129.
[†] The hysterical attack is not a purely psychical process. By the psychic processes only a pre-formed mechanism is set free, which has nothing to do with psychic processes in and for themselves (Karplus, *Jahr. f. Psych.*, XVII.).

VII

RELATIONSHIP TO THE
UNCONSCIOUS PERSONALITY

AS we have seen, the numerous personalities
become grouped round two types, the grandfather and Ulrich von Gerbenstein. The first
produces exclusively sanctimonious religiosity and gives edifying moral precepts. The latter is, in one word, a "flapper," in whom there
is nothing male except the name. We must
here add from the anamnesis that at fifteen the
patient was confirmed by a very bigoted clergyman, and at home she is occasionally the re-
cipient of sanctimonious moral talks. The
grandfather represents this side of her past,
Gerbenstein the other half; hence the curious
contrast. Here we have personified the chief
characteristics of her past. On the one hand
the sanctimonious person with a narrow education, on the other the boisterousness of a
lively girl of fifteen who often overshoots the
mark.° We find both sets of traits mixed in the
patient in sharp contrast. At times she is

° Carl Hauptmann, in his drama "Die Berg-
schmiede," has made use of the objectivation of
certain linked association-complexes. In this play
the treasure-seeker is met on a gloomy night by a
hallucination of his entire better self.

anxious, shy, and extremely reserved; at others boisterous to a degree. She is herself often most painfully aware of these contradictions. This circumstance gives us the key to the source of the two unconscious personalities. The patient is obviously seeking a middle path between the two extremes; she endeavours to repress them and strains after some ideal condition. These strainings bring her to the puberty dream of the ideal Ivenes, beside whose figure the unacknowledged trends of her character recede into the background. They are not lost, however, but as repressed ideas, analogous to the Ivenes idea, begin an independent existence as automatic personalities.

S. W.'s behaviour recalls vividly Freud's° investigations into dreams which disclose the independent growth of repressed thoughts. We can now comprehend why the hallucinatory persons are separated from those who write and speak automatically. The former teach Ivenes the secrets of the Other Side, they relate all those phantastic tales about the extraordinariness of her personality, they create scenes where Ivenes can appear dramatically with the attributes of power, wisdom and virtue. These are nothing but dramatic dissociations of her dream-self.

° Freud, "The Interpretation of Dreams." See also Breuer and Freud's "Studies on Hysteria," 1895.

The latter, the automatic persons, are the ones to be overcome, they must have no part in Ivenes. With the spirit-companions of Ivenes they have only the name in common. *A priori,* it is not to be expected that in a case like ours, where these divisions are never clearly defined, that two such characteristic individualities should disappear entirely from a somnambulic ego-complex having so close a relation with the waking consciousness. And in fact, we do meet them in part in those ecstatic penitential scenes and in part in the romances crammed with more or less banal, mischievous gossip.

VIII

COURSE

IT only remains to say a few words about the course of this strange affection. The process reached its maximum in four to eight weeks. The descriptions given of Ivenes and of the unconscious personalities belong generally to this period. Thenceforth a gradual decline was noticeable; the ecstasies grew meaningless and the influence of Gerbenstein became more powerful. The phenomena gradually lost their distinctive features, the characters which were at first well demarcated became by degrees inextricably mixed. The psychological contribution grew smaller and smaller until finally the whole story assumed a marked effect of fabrication. Ivenes herself was much concerned about this decline; she became painfully uncertain, spoke cautiously, feeling her way, and allowed her character to appear undisguised. The somnambulic attacks decreased in frequency and intensity. All degrees from somnambulism to conscious lying were observable. Thus the curtain fell. The patient has since gone abroad. We should not underestimate the importance of the fact that her character has become pleasanter and more stable. Here we may recall the cases cited in which the second state gradually replaced the first state. Perhaps this is a similar phenomenon.

It is well known that somnambulic manifestations sometimes begin at puberty.[*] The attacks of somnambulism in Dyce's case[†] began immediately before puberty and lasted just till its termination. The somnambulism of H. Smith is likewise closely connected with puberty.[‡]

Schroeder von der Kalk's patient was 16 years old at the time of her illness; Felida 14-1/2, etc. We know also that at this period the future character is formed and fixed. In the case of Felida and of Mary Reynolds we saw that the character in state II. replaced that of state I. *It is not therefore unthinkable that these phenomena of double consciousness are nothing but character-formations for the future personality, or their attempts to burst forth.* In consequence of special difficulties (unfavourable external conditions, psychopathic disposition of the nervous system, etc.), *these new formations, or attempts thereat, become bound up with peculiar disturbances of consciousness.* Occasionally the somnambulism, in view of the difficulties that oppose the future character, takes on a marked teleological meaning, for it gives the

---

[*] Pelman, *Allg. Zeit. f. Psych.*, XXI., p. 74.

[†] *Allg. Zeit. f. Psych.*, XXII., p. 407.

[‡] Flournoy, *l.c.*, p. 28

individual, who might otherwise be defeated, the means of victory. Here I am thinking first of all of Jeanne d'Arc, whose extraordinary courage recalls the deeds of Mary Reynolds' II. This is perhaps the place to point out the similar function of the "hallucination téléologique" of which the public reads occasionally, although it has not yet been submitted to a scientific study.

IX

THE UNCONSCIOUS ADDITIONAL CREATIVE WORK

WE have now discussed all the essential manifestations offered by our case which are of significance for its inner structure. Certain accompanying manifestations may be briefly considered: *the unconscious additional creative work*. Here we shall encounter a not altogether unjustifiable scepticism on the part of the representative of science. Dessoir's conception of a second ego met with much opposition, and was rejected, as too impossible in many directions. As is known, occultism has proclaimed a pre-eminent right to this field and has drawn premature conclusions from doubtful observations. We are indeed very far from being in a position to state anything conclusive, since we have at present only most inadequate material. Therefore if we touch on the field of the unconscious additional creative work, it is only that we may do justice to all sides of our case. *By unconscious addition we understand that automatic process whose result does not penetrate to the conscious psychic activity of the individual.* To this region above all belongs thought-reading through table movements. I do not know whether there are people who can divine a

whole long train of thought by means of in-
ductions from the intentional tremulous
movements. It is, however, certain that, as-
suming this to be possible, such persons must
be availing themselves of a routine achieved
after endless practice. But in our case long
practice can be excluded without more ado,
and there is nothing left but to accept a primary susceptibility of the unconscious, far ex-
ceeding that of the conscious.

This supposition is supported by numerous
observations on somnambulists. I will men-
tion only Binet's° experiments, where little
letters or some such thing, or little complicated figures in relief were laid on the
anæsthetic skin of the back of the hand or the
neck, and the unconscious perceptions were
then recorded by means of signs. A second additional creation coming under consideration
in our case and in numerous other somnambulists, is that condition which French inves-
tigators call "cryptomnesia."† By this term is
meant the becoming conscious of a memory-

° Binet, "Les Altérations," p. 125. Cf. also Loewenfeld's statements on the subject in "Hypnotismus," 1901.
† *Cryptomnesia* must not be regarded as synony-
mous with *Hypermnesia*; by the latter term is
meant the abnormal quickening of the power of
recollection which reproduces the memory-pic-
tures as such.

picture which cannot be regarded as in itself primary, but at most is secondary, by means of subsequent recalling or abstract reasoning. It is characteristic of cryptomnesia that the picture which emerges does not bear the obvious mark of the memory-picture, is not, that is to say, bound up with the idiosyncratic super-conscious ego-complex.

Three ways may be distinguished in which the cryptomnesic picture is brought to consciousness.

1. *The picture enters consciousness without any intervention of the sense-spheres (intra-psychically).* It is an inrushing idea whose causal sequence is hidden within the individual. In so far cryptomnesia is quite an everyday occurrence, concerned with the deepest normal psychic events. How often it misleads the investigator, the author or the composer into believing his ideas original, whilst the critic quite well recognises their source! Generally the individuality of the representation protects the author from the accusation of plagiarism and proves his good faith; still, cases do occur of unconscious verbal reproduction. Should the passage in question contain some remarkable idea, the accusation of plagiarism, more or less conscious, is justified. After all, a valuable idea is linked by numerous associations with the ego-complex; at different times, in different situations, it has already been meditated

upon and thus leads by innumerable links in all directions. It can therefore never so disappear from consciousness that its continuity could be entirely lost from the sphere of conscious memory. We have, however, a criterion by which we can always recognise objectively intra-psychic cryptomnesia. The cryptomnesic presentation is linked to the ego-complex by the minimum of associations. The reason for this lies in the relation of the individual to the particular object, in the disproportion of interest to object. Two possibilities occur: (1) The object is worthy of interest but the interest is slight in consequence of dispersion or want of understanding; (2) The object is not worthy of interest, consequently the interest is slight. In both cases an extremely labile connection with consciousness arises which leads to a rapid forgetting. The slight bridge is soon destroyed and the acquired presentation sinks into the unconscious, where it is no longer accessible to consciousness. Should it enter consciousness by means of cryptomnesia, the feeling of strangeness, of its being an original creation, will cling to it because the path by which it entered the subconscious has become undiscoverable. Strangeness and original creation are, moreover, closely allied to one another if one recalls the numerous witnesses in

Belleslettres to the nature of genius ("possession" by genius).[°]

Apart from certain striking cases of this
kind, where it is doubtful whether it is a cryptomnesia or an original creation, there are
some cases in which a passage of no essential
content is reproduced, and that almost ver-
bally, as in the following example:—

> *About that time when Zarathustra
> lived on the blissful islands, it came to
> pass that a ship cast anchor at that island
> on which the smoking mountain standeth;
> and the sailors of that ship went ashore in
> order to shoot rabbits! But about the hour
> of noon, when the captain and his men had*

[°] "Has any one at the end of the nineteenth century any clear conception of what the poets in
vigorous ages called inspiration? If not, I will describe it. The slight remnant of superstition by itself would scarcely have sufficed to reject the
idea of being merely incarnation, merely mouth-
piece, merely the medium of superior forces. The
concept revelation in the sense that quite suddenly, with ineffable certainty and delicacy,
something is seen, something is heard, something
convulsing and breaking into one's inmost self,
does but describe the fact. You hear—you do not
seek; you accept—asking not who is the giver.
Like lightning, flashes the thought, compelling
without hesitation as to form—I have had no
choice" (Nietzsche's "Works," vol. III., p. 482.).

mustered again, they suddenly saw a man come through the air unto them, and a voice said distinctly: "It is time! It is high time!" But when that person was nighest unto them (he passed by them flying quickly like a shadow, in the direction in which the volcano was situated) they recognised with the greatest confusion that it was Zarathustra. For all of them, except the captain, had seen him before, and they loved him, as the folk love, blending love and awe in equal parts. "Lo! there," said the old steersman, "Zarathustra goeth unto hell!"

An extract of awe-inspiring import from the log of the ship "Sphinx" in the year 1686, in the Mediterranean.

Just. Kerner, "Blätter aus Prevorst," vol. IV., p, 57.

The four captains and a merchant, Mr. Bell, went ashore on the island of Mount Stromboli to shoot rabbits. At three o'clock they called the crew together to go aboard, when, to their inexpressible astonishment, they saw two men flying rapidly over them through the air. One was dressed in black, the other in grey. They approached them very closely, in the greatest haste; to their greatest dismay they descended amid the burning flames into the crater of the terrible volcano,

*Mount Stromboli. They recognised the
pair as acquaintances from London.*

Frau E. Förster-Nietzsche, the poet's sister, told me, in reply to my inquiry, that Nietzsche took up Just. Kerner between the age
of twelve and fifteen, when stopping with his
grandfather, Pastor Oehler, in Pobler, but
certainly never afterwards. It could never
have been the poet's intention to commit a plagiarism from a ship's log; if this had been the
case, he would certainly have omitted the very
prosaic "to shoot rabbits," which was, moreover, quite unessential to the situation. In the
poetical sketch of Zarathustra's journey into
Hell there was obviously interpolated, half or
wholly unconsciously, that forgotten impression from his youth.

This is an instance which shows all the peculiarities of cryptomnesia. A quite unessential detail, which deserves nothing but speedy
forgetting, is reproduced with almost verbal
fidelity, whilst the chief part of the narrative
is, one cannot say altered, but recreated quite
distinctively. To the distinctive core, the idea
of the journey to Hell, there is added a detail,
the old, forgotten impression of a similar situation. The original is so absurd that the youth,
who read everything, probably skipped
through it, and certainly had no deep interest
in it. Here we get the required minimum of associated links, for we cannot easily conceive a

greater jump, than from that old, absurd story to Nietzsche's consciousness in the year 1883. If we picture to ourselves Nietzsche's mood at the time when "Zarathustra" was composed,* and think of the ecstasy that at more than one point approached the pathological, we shall comprehend the abnormal reminiscence. The second of the two possibilities mentioned, the acceptance of some object, not itself uninteresting, in a state of dispersion or half interest from lack of understanding, and its cryptomnesic reproduction we find chiefly in somnambulists; it is also found in the literary chronicles dealing with dying celebrities.†

---

* "There is an ecstasy so great that the immense strain of it is sometimes relaxed by a flood of tears, during which one's steps now involuntarily rush, and anon involuntarily lag. There is the feeling that one is utterly out of hand, with the very distinct consciousness of an endless number of fine thrills and titillations descending to one's very toes; — there is a depth of happiness in which the most painful and gloomy parts do not act as antitheses to the rest, but are produced and required as necessary shades of colour in such an overflow of light" (Nietzsche, "Ecce Homo," vol. XVII. of English translation, by A. M. Ludovici, p. 103).

† Eckermann, "Conversations with Goethe," vol. III.

Amid the exhaustive selection of these phenomena we are chiefly concerned with *talking in a foreign tongue, the so-called glossolalia*. This phenomenon is mentioned everywhere when it is a question of similar ecstatic conditions. In the New Testament, in the *Acta Sanctorum*,[*] in the Witchcraft Trials, more recently in the Prophetess of Prevorst, in Judge Edmond's daughter Laura, in Flournoy's Helen Smith. The last is unique from the point of view of investigation; it is found also in Bresler's[†] case, which is probably identical with Blumhardt's[‡] Gottlieben Dittus. As Flournoy shows, glossolalia is, so far as it really is independent speech, a cryptomnesic phenomenon, [Greek: Kat' exochên]. The reader should consult Flournoy's most interesting exposition.

In our case glossolalia was only once observed, when the only understandable words were the scattered variations on the word "vena." The source of this word is clear. A few days previously the patient had dipped into an anatomical atlas for the study of the veins of the face, which were given in Latin. She had used the word "vena" in her dreams, as

---

[*] Cf. Goerres, "Die christliche Mystik."

[†] Bresler, "Kulturhistorischer Beitrag zur Hysterie," *Allg. Zeits. f. Psych.* LIII., p. 333.

[‡] Zündel, "Biographie Blumhardt's."

happens occasionally to normal persons. The remaining words and sentences in a foreign language betray, at the first glance, their derivation from French, in which the patient was somewhat fluent. Unfortunately I am without the more accurate translations of the various sentences, because the patient would not give them; but we may hold that it was a phenomenon similar to Helen Smith's Martian language. Flournoy found that the Martian language was nothing but a childish translation from French; the words were changed but the syntax remained the same. Even more probable is the view that the patient simply ranged next to each other meaningless words that rang strangely, without any true word-formation;[*] she borrowed certain characteristic sounds from French and Italian and combined them into a kind of language, just as Helen Smith completed the *lacunæ* in the real Sanscrit words by products of her own resembling that language. The curious names of the mystical system can be reduced, for the most part, to known roots. The writer vividly recalls the botanical schemes found in every school atlas; the internal resemblance of the relationship of the planets to the sun is also pretty clear; we shall not be going astray if we see in the names reminiscences from popular

---

[*] Flournoy, l.c. p. 152.

astronomy. Thus can be explained the names Persus, Fenus, Nenus, Sirum, Surus, Fixus, and Pix, as the childlike distortions of Perseus, Venus, Sirius and Fixed Star, analogous to the Vena variations. Magnesor vividly recalls Magnetism, whose mystic significance the patient knew from the Prophetess of Prevorst. In Connesor, the contrary to Magnesor, the prefix "con" is probably the French "contre." Hypnos and Hyfonismus recall hypnosis and hypnotism (German *hypnotismus*), about which there are the most superstitious ideas circulating in lay circles. The most used suffixes in "us" and "os" are the signs by which as a rule people decide the difference between Latin and Greek. The other names probably spring from similar accidents to which we have no clues. The rudimentary glossolalia of our case has not any title to be a classical instance of cryptomnesia, for it only consisted in the unconscious use of various impressions, partly optical, party acoustic, and all very close at hand.

2. *The cryptomnesic image arrives at consciousness through the senses (as a hallucination).* Helen Smith is the classic example of this kind. I refer to the case mentioned on the date "18 Mars."

3. *The image arrives at consciousness by motor automatism.* H. Smith had lost her valuable brooch, which she was anxiously looking for

everywhere. Ten days later her guide Leopold informed her by means of the table where the brooch was. Thus informed, she found it at night-time in the open field, covered by sand.° Strictly speaking, in cryptomnesia there is not any additional creation in the true sense of the word, since the conscious memory experiences no increase of its function, but only an enrichment of its content. By the automatism certain regions are merely made accessible to consciousness in an indirect way, which were formerly sealed against it. But the unconscious does not thereby accomplish any creation which exceeds the capacity of consciousness qualitatively or quantitatively. Cryptomnesia is only an apparent additional creation, in contrast to hypermnesia, which actually represents an increase of function.†

We have spoken above of a receptivity of the unconscious greater than that of the consciousness, chiefly in regard to the simple attempts at thought-reading of numbers. As mentioned, not only our somnambulist but a relatively large number of normal persons are able to guess from the tremors lengthy thought-sequences, if they are not too

---

° Flournoy, *l.c.*, p. 378.
† For a case of this kind see Krafft Ebing, "Lehrbuch," 4th edition, p. 578.

complicated. These experiments are, so to speak, the prototype of those rarer and incomparably more astonishing cases of intuitive knowledge displayed at times by somnambulists.[°] Zschokke[†] in his "Introspection" has shown us that these phenomena do not belong only to the domain of somnambulism, but occur among non-somnambulic persons. The formation of such knowledge seems to be arrived at in various ways: first and foremost there is the fineness, already noted, of unconscious perceptions; then must be emphasised the importance of the enormous suggestibility of somnambulists. *The somnambulist not only incorporates every suggestive idea to some extent, but actually lives in the suggestion, in the person of his doctor or observer, with that abandonment characteristic of the suggestible hysteric.* The relation of Frau Hauffe to Kerner is a striking example of this. That in such cases there is a high degree of *association-concordance* can cause no astonishment; a condition which Richet might have taken more account of in his experiments

---

[°] The limitation of the associative processes and the concentration of attention upon a definite sphere of presentation can also lead to the development of new ideas, which no effort of will in the waking state would have been able to accomplish (Loewenfeld, "Hypnotismus," p. 289).
[†] Zschokke, "Eine Selbstschau," III., Aufl. Aarau, 1843, p. 227 ff.

in thought-transference. Finally there are cases of somnambulic additional creative work which are not to be explained solely by hyperæsthesia of the unconscious activity of the senses and association-concordance, but presuppose a highly developed intellectual activity of the unconscious. The deciphering of the purposive tremors demand an extreme sensitiveness and delicacy of feeling, both psychological and physiological, to combine the individual perceptions into a complete unity of thought, if it is at all permissible to make an analogy between the processes of cognition in the realm of the unconscious and the conscious. The possibility must always be considered that *in the unconscious, feeling and concept are not clearly separated*, perhaps even are one. The intellectual elevation which certain somnambulists display in ecstasy, though a rare thing, is none the less one that has sometimes been observed.* I would designate the scheme composed by our patient as just one of those pieces of creative work that exceed the normal

---

* Gilles de la Tourette says, "We have seen somnambulic girls, poor, uneducated, quite stupid in the waking state, whose whole appearance altered so soon as they were sent to sleep. Whilst previously they were boring, now they are lively, alert, sometimes even witty" (Cf. Loewenfeld, *l.c.*, p. 132).

intelligence. We have already seen whence one portion of this scheme probably came. A second source is no doubt the life-crisis of Frau Hauffe, portrayed in Kerner's book. The external form seems to be determined by these adventitious facts. As already observed in the presentation of the case, the idea of dualism arises from the conversations picked up piece-meal by the patient during those dreamy states occurring after her ecstasies. This exhausts my knowledge of the sources of S. W.'s creations. Whence arose the root-idea the patient is unable to say. I naturally examined occultistic literature pertinent to the subject, and discovered a store of parallels with her gnostic system from different centuries scattered through all kinds of work mostly quite inaccessible to the patient. Moreover, at her youthful age, and with her surroundings, the possibility of any such study is quite excluded. A brief survey of the system in the light of her own explanations shows how much intelligence was used in its construction. How highly the intellectual work is to be estimated is a matter of opinion. In any case, considering her youth, her mentality must be regarded as quite extraordinary.

APPENDIX

The Case of Miss Elise K.

AGED 40, single; book-keeper in a large business; no hereditary taint, except that it is alleged a brother became slightly nervous after family misfortune and illness. Well educated, of a cheerful, joyous nature, not of a saving disposition, always occupied with some big idea. She was very kind-hearted and gentle, did a great deal both for her parents, who were living in very modest circumstances, and for strangers. Nevertheless she was not happy, because she thought she did not understand herself. She had always enjoyed good health till a few years ago, when she is said to have been treated for dilatation of the stomach and tapeworm. During this illness her hair became rapidly white, later she had typhoid fever. An engagement was terminated by the death of her fiancé from paralysis. She had been very nervous for a year and a half. In the summer of 1897 she went away for change of air and treatment by hydropathy. She herself says that for about a year she has had moments during work when her thoughts seem to stand still, but she does not fall asleep. Nevertheless she makes no mistakes in the accounts at such times. She has often been to the

wrong street and then suddenly noticed that
she was not in the right place. She has had no
giddiness or attacks of fainting. Formerly
menstruation occurred regularly every four
weeks, and without any pain, but since she
has been nervous and overworked it has come
every fourteen days. For a long time she has
suffered from constant headache. As account-
ant and book-keeper in a large establishment,
the patient has had very strenuous work,
which she performs well and conscientiously.
In addition to the strenuous character of her
work, in the last year she had various new
worries. Her brother was suddenly di-
vorced. In addition to her own work, she
looked after his housekeeping, nursed him
and his child in a serious illness, and so on. To
recuperate, she took a journey on the 13th
September to see a woman friend in South
Germany. The great joy at seeing her friend
from whom she had been long separated, and
her participation in some festivities, deprived
her of her rest. On the 15th, she and her friend
drank half a bottle of claret. This was contrary
to her usual habit. They then went for a walk
in a cemetery, where she began to tear up
flowers and to scratch at the graves. She remembered absolutely nothing of this afterwards. On the 16th she remained with her
friend without anything of importance hap-
pening. On the 17th her friend brought her to

Zürich. An acquaintance came with her to the Asylum; on the way she spoke quite sensibly, but was very tired. Outside the Asylum they met three boys, whom she described as the "three dead people she had dug up." She then wanted to go to the neighbouring cemetery, but was persuaded to come to the Asylum.

She is small, delicately formed, slightly anæmic. The heart is slightly enlarged to the left, there are no murmurs, but some reduplication of the sounds, the mitral being markedly accentuated. The liver dulness reaches to the border of the ribs. Patella-reflex is somewhat increased, but otherwise no tendon-reflexes. There is neither anæsthesia, analgesia, nor paralysis. Rough examination of the field of vision with the hands shows no contraction. The patient's hair is a very light yellow-white colour; on the whole she looks her age. She gives her history and tells recent events quite clearly, but has no recollection of what took place in the cemetery at C. or outside the Asylum. During the night of the 17th-18th she spoke to the attendant and declared she saw the whole room full of dead people—looking like skeletons. She was not at all frightened, but was rather surprised that the attendant did not see them too. Once she ran to the window, but was otherwise quiet. The next morning, while still in bed, she saw skeletons, but not in the afternoon. The following night at four o'clock she awoke and heard the dead children in the neighbouring cemetery cry out that they had been buried alive. She wanted to go out to dig them up, but allowed herself to be restrained. Next morning at seven o'clock she was still delirious, but recalled accurately the events in the cemetery at C. and those on approaching the Asylum. She stated that at C. she wanted to dig up the dead children who were calling her. She had only torn up the flowers to free the graves and to be able to get at them. In this state Professor Bleuler explained to her that later on, when in a normal state again, she would remember everything. The patient slept in the morning, afterwards was quite clear, and felt herself relatively well. She did indeed remember the attacks, but maintained a remarkable indifference towards them. The following nights, with the exception of those of the 22nd and the 25th September, she again had slight attacks of delirium, when once more she had to deal with the dead. The details of the attacks differed, however. Twice she saw the dead in her bed, but she did not appear to be afraid of them, she got out of bed frequently, however, because she did not want "to inconvenience the dead"; several times she wanted to leave the room.

After a few nights free from attacks there was a slight one on the 30th Sept., when she called the dead from the window. During the day her mind was clear. On the 3rd of October she saw a whole crowd of skeletons in the drawingroom, as she afterwards related, during full consciousness. Although she doubted the reality of the skeletons, she could not convince herself that it was a hallucination. The following night, between twelve and one o'clock—the earlier attacks were usually about this time—she was obsessed with the idea of dead people for about ten minutes. She sat up in bed, stared at a corner and said: "Well, come!—but they're not all there. Come along! Why don't you come? The room is big enough, there's room for all; when all are there, I'll come too." Then she lay down with the words: "Now they're all there," and fell asleep again. In the morning she had not the slightest recollection of any of these attacks. Very short attacks occurred in the nights of the 4th, 6th, 9th, 13th and 15th of October, between twelve and one o'clock. The last three occurred during the menstrual period. The attendant spoke to her several times, showed her the lighted street-lamps, and trees; but she did not react to this conversation. Since then the attacks have altogether ceased. The patient has complained about a number of troubles which she had had all along. She suffered much from headache the morning after the attacks. She said it was unbearable. Five grains of Sacch. lactis promptly alleviated this; then she complained of pains in both fore-arms, which she described as if it were a teno-synovitis. She regarded the bulging of the muscles in flexion as a swelling, and asked to be massaged. Nothing could be seen objectively, and no attention being paid to it, the trouble disappeared. She complained exceedingly and for a long time about the thickening of a toenail, even after the thickened part had been removed. Sleep was often disturbed. She would not give her consent to be hypnotised for the night-attacks. Finally on account of headache and disturbed sleep she agreed to hypnotic treatment. She proved a good subject, and at the first sitting fell into deep sleep with analgesia and amnesia.

In November she was again asked whether she could now remember the attack on the 19th September which it had been suggested that she would recall. It gave her great trouble to recollect it, and in the end she could only state the chief facts, she had forgotten the details.

It should be added that the patient was not superstitious, and in her healthy days had never particularly interested herself in the supernatural. During the whole course of treatment, which ended on the 14th November, great indifference was evinced both to the illness and the cure. Next spring the patient returned for out-patient treatment of the headache, which had come back during the very hard work of these months. Apart from this symptom her condition left nothing to be desired. It was demonstrated that she had no remembrance of the attacks of the previous autumn, not even of those of the 19th September and earlier. On the other hand, in hypnosis she could recount the proceedings in the cemetery and during the nightly disturbances.

By the peculiar hallucination and by its appearance our case recalls the conditions which V. Kraft-Ebing has described as "protracted states of hysterical delirium." He says: "Such conditions of delirium occur in the slighter cases of hysteria. Protracted hysterical delirium is built upon a foundation of temporary exhaustion. Excitement seems to determine an outbreak, and it readily recurs. Most frequently there is persecution-delirium with very violent anxiety, sometimes of a religious or erotic character. Hallucinations of all the senses are not rare, but illusions of sight, smell and feeling are the commonest, and most important. The visual hallucinations are especially visions of animals, pictures of corpses, phantastic processions in which dead persons, devils and ghosts swarm. The illusions of hearing are simply sounds (shrieks, howlings, claps of thunder) or local hallucinations, frequently with a sexual content."

This patient's visions of corpses, occurring almost always in attacks, recall the states occasionally seen in hystero-epilepsy. There likewise occur specific visions which, in contrast with protracted delirium, are connected with single attacks.

(1) A lady 30 years of age with *grande hystérie* had twilight states in which as a rule she was troubled by terrible hallucinations; she saw her children carried away from her, wild beasts eating them up, and so on. She has amnesia for the content of the individual attacks.°

(2) A girl of 17, likewise a semi-hysteric, saw in her attacks the corpse of her dead mother approaching her to draw her to her. Patient has amnesia for the attacks.†

These are cases of severe hysteria wherein consciousness rests upon a profound stage of dreaming. The nature of the attack and the stability of the hallucination alone show a certain kinship with our case, which in this respect has numerous analogies with the

---

° Richer, "Études cliniques sur l'hystéro-épilepsie," p. 483.
† *Idem, l.c.*, p. 487; cp. also Erler, *Allg. Zeitschrift f. Psychiatrie*, XXXV. p. 28; also Culerre, *Allg. Zeit. f. Psych.*, XLVI., Litteraturbericht 356.

corresponding states of hysteria. For instance, with those cases where a psychical shock (rape, etc.) was the occasion for the outbreak of hysterical attacks, and where at times the original incident is lived over again, stereotyped in the hallucination. But our case gets its specific mould from the identity of the consciousness in the different attacks. It is an "Etat Second" with its own memory and separated from the waking state by complete amnesia. This differentiates it from the above-mentioned twilight states and links it to the so-called somnambulic conditions.

Charcot° divides the somnambulic states into two chief classes:—

1. Delirium with well-marked incoordination of representation and action.

2. Delirium with co-ordinated action. This approaches the waking state.

Our case belongs to the latter class.

If by somnambulism be understood a state of systematised partial waking,† any critical

---

° Charcot and Guinon, "Progrès méd.," 1891.

† "Somnambulism must be conceived as systematised partial waking, in which a limited, connected presentation-complex takes place. Contrary presentations do not occur, at the same time the mental activity is carried on with increased energy within the limited sphere of the waking" (Lowenfeld, "Hypnotism," 1901, p. 289).

review of this affection must take account of those exceptional cases of recurrent amnesias which have been observed now and again. These, apart from nocturnal ambulism, are the simplest conditions of systematised partial waking. Naef's case is certainly the most remarkable in the literature. It deals with a gentleman of 32, with a very bad family history presenting numerous signs of degeneration, partly functional, partly organic. In consequence of over-work at the age of 17 he had a peculiar twilight state with delusions, which lasted some days and was cured with a sudden recovery of memory. Later he was subject to frequent attacks of giddiness and palpitation of the heart and vomiting; but these attacks were never attended by loss of consciousness. At the termination of some feverish illness he suddenly travelled from Australia to Zürich, where he lived for some weeks in careless cheerfulness, and only came to himself when he read in the paper of his sudden disappearance from Australia. He had a total and retrograde amnesia for the several months which included the journey to Australia, his sojourn there and the return journey.

Azam[°] has published a case of periodic amnesia. Albert X., 12-1/2 years old, of hysterical disposition, was several times attacked in the course of a few years by conditions of amnesia in which he forgot reading, writing and arithmetic, even at times his own language, for several weeks at a stretch. The intervals were normal.

Proust[†] has published a case of *automatisme ambulatoire* with pronounced hysteria which differs from Naef's in the repeated occurrence of the attacks. An educated man, 30 years old, exhibits all the signs of *grande hystérie;* he is very suggestible, has from time to time, under the influence of excitement, attacks of amnesia which last from two days to several weeks. During these states he wanders about, visits relatives, destroys various objects, incurs debts, and has even been convicted of "picking pockets."

Boileau describes a similar case[‡] of wandering-impulse. A widow of 22, highly hysterical, became terrified at the prospect of a necessary operation for salpingitis; she left the hospital and fell into a state of somnambulism,

---

[°] Azam, "Hypnotisme — Double conscience," etc., Paris, 1887. For similar cases, cf. Forbes Winslow, "On Obscure Diseases," p. 335.

[†] *Trib. méd.*, March, 1890.

[‡] *Annal. méd. psychol.*, Jan., Feb., 1892.

from which she awoke three days later with total amnesia. During these three days she had travelled a distance of about 60 kilometres to fetch her child.

William James has described a case of an "ambulatory sort."[*]

The Rev. Ansel Bourne, an itinerant preacher, 30 years of age, psychopathic, had on a few occasions attacks of loss of consciousness lasting one hour. One day (January 17, 1887) he suddenly disappeared from Greene, after having taken 551 dollars out of the bank. He remained hidden for two months. During this time he had taken a little shop under the name of H. J. Browne in Norriston, Pa., and had carefully attended to all purchases, although he had never done this sort of work before. On March 14, 1887, he suddenly awoke and went back home, and had complete amnesia for the interval.

Mesnet[†] publishes the following case: —

F., 27 years old, sergeant in the African regiment, was wounded in the parietal bone at

---

[*] "Principles of Psychology," p. 391.
[†] Mesnet, "De l'automatisme de la mémoire et du souvenir dans le somnambulisme pathologique." Union médicale, Juillet, 1874. Cf. Binet, "Les Altérations de la personnalité," p. 37. Cf. also Mesnet, "Somnambulisme spontané dans ses rapports avec l'hystérie," *Arch. de Neurol.*, Nr. 69, 1892.

Bazeilles. Suffered for a year from hemiplegia, which disappeared when the wound healed. During the course of his illness the patient had attacks of somnambulism, with marked limitation of consciousness; all the senses were paralysed, with the exception of taste and a small portion of the visual sense. The movements were co-ordinated, but obstacles in the way of their performance were overcome with difficulty. During the attacks he had an absurd collecting-mania. By various manipulations one could demonstrate a hallucinatory content in his consciousness; for instance, when a stick was put in his hand he would feel himself transported to a battle scene, would place himself on guard, see the enemy approaching, etc.

Guinon and Sophie Waltke[°] made the following experiments on hysterics:—

A blue glass was held in front of the eyes of a female patient during a hysterical attack; she regularly saw the picture of her mother in the blue sky. A red glass showed her a bleeding wound, a yellow one an orange-seller or a lady with a yellow dress.

Mesnet's case reminds one of the cases of occasional attacks of shrinkage of memory.

MacNish[†] communicates a similar case.

[°] *Arch. de Neur.*, Mai, 1891.
[†] "Philosophy of Sleep," 1830.

An apparently healthy young lady suddenly fell into an abnormally long and deep sleep—it is said without prodromal symptoms. On awaking she had forgotten the words for and the knowledge of the simplest things. She had again to learn to read, write, and count; her progress was rapid in this re-learning. After a second attack she again woke in her normal state, but without recollection of the period when she had forgotten things. These states alternated for more than four years, during which consciousness showed continuity within the two states, but was separated by an amnesia from the consciousness of the normal state.

These selected cases of various forms of changes of consciousness all throw a certain light upon our case. Naef's case presents two hysteriform eclipses of memory, one of which is marked by the appearance of delusions, and the other by its long duration, contraction of the field of consciousness, and desire to wander. The peculiar associated impulses are specially clear in the cases of Proust and Mesnet. In our case the impulsive tearing up of the flowers, the digging up of the graves, form a parallel. The continuity of consciousness which the patient presents in the individual attacks recalls the behaviour of the consciousness in MacNish's case; hence our case may be regarded as a transient phenomenon of

alternating consciousness. The dreamlike hallucinatory content of the limited consciousness in our case does not, however, justify an
unqualified assignment to this group of *double
consciousness*. The hallucinations in the second
state show a certain creativeness which seems
to be conditioned by the auto-suggestibility of
this state. In Mesnet's case we noticed the appearance of hallucinatory processes from simple stimulation of touch. The patient's subconsciousness employs simple perceptions for the
automatic construction of complicated scenes
which then take possession of the limited consciousness. A somewhat similar view must be
taken about our patient's hallucinations; at
least, the external conditions which gave rise
to the appearance of the hallucinations seem
to strengthen our supposition. The walk in the
cemetery induces the vision of the skeletons;
the meeting with the three boys arouses the
hallucination of children buried alive whose
voices the patient hears at night-time. She arrived at the cemetery in a somnambulic state,
which on this occasion was specially intense
in consequence of her having taken alcohol.
She performed actions almost instinctively
about which her subconsciousness nevertheless did receive certain impressions. (The part
played here by alcohol must not be underestimated. We know from experience that it does
not only act adversely upon these conditions,

but, like every other narcotic, it gives rise to a certain increase of suggestibility.) The impressions received in somnambulism subconsciously form independent growths, and finally reach perception as hallucinations. Thus our case closely corresponds to those somnambulic dream-states which have recently been subjected to a penetrating study in England and France.

These lapses of memory, which at first seem without content, gain a content by means of accidental auto-suggestion, and this content builds itself up automatically to a certain extent. It achieves no further development, probably on account of the improvement now beginning, and finally it disappears altogether as recovery sets in. Binet and Féré have made numerous experiments on the implanting of suggestions in states of partial sleep. They have shown, for example, that when a pencil is put in the anæsthetic hand of a hysteric, letters of great length are written automatically whose contents are unknown to the patient's consciousness. Cutaneous stimuli in anæsthetic regions are sometimes perceived as visual images, or at least as vivid associated visual presentations. These independent transmutations of simple stimuli must be regarded as primary phenomena in the formation of somnambulic dream-pictures. Analogous manifestations occur in exceptional

cases within the sphere of waking consciousness. Goethe,[°] for instance, states that when
he sat down, lowered his head and vividly
conjured up the image of a flower, he saw it
undergoing changes of its own accord, as if
entering into new combinations.

In half-waking states these manifestations
are relatively frequent in the so-called hypnagogic hallucinations. The automatisms which
the Goethe example illustrates are differentiated from the truly somnambulic, inasmuch as
the primary presentation is a conscious one in
this case; the further development of the automatism is maintained within the definite
limits of the original presentation, that is,
within the purely motor or visual region.

[°] Goethe: *Zur Naturwissenschaft in Allgemeinen*. "I
was able, when I closed my eyes and bent my
head, to conjure the imaginary picture of a
flower. This flower did not retain its first shape
for a single instant, but unfolded out of itself new
flowers composed of coloured petals and green
leaves. They were not natural flowers, but phantastic ones. They were as regular in shape as a
sculptor's rosettes. It was impossible to fix the
creation which sprang up, nevertheless the
dream-image lasted as long as I desired it to last;
it neither faded nor grew stronger."

If the primary presentation disappears, or if it is never conscious at all, and if the automatic development overlaps neighbouring regions, we lose every possibility of a demarcation between waking automatisms and those of the somnambulic state; this will occur, for instance, if the presentation of a hand plucking the flower gets joined to the perception of the flower or the presentation of the smell of the flower. We can then only differentiate it by the more or less. In one case we then speak of the "waking hallucinations of the normal," in the other, of the dream-vision of the somnambulists. The interpretation of our patient's attacks as hysterical becomes more certain by the demonstration of a probably psychogenic origin of the hallucination. This is confirmed by her troubles, headache and teno-synovitis, which have shown themselves amenable to suggestive treatment. The ætiological factor alone is not sufficient for the diagnosis of hysteria; it might really be expected *a priori* that in the course of a disease which is so suitably treated by rest, as in the treatment of an exhaustion-state, features would be observed here and there which could be interpreted as manifestations of exhaustion. The question arises whether the early lapses and later somnambulic attacks could not be conceived as states of exhaustion, so-called "neurasthenic crises." We know that in the realm of psychopathic mental deficiency there can arise the most diverse epileptoid accidents, whose classification under epilepsy or hysteria is at least doubtful. To quote C. Westphal: "On the basis of numerous observations, I maintain that the so-called epileptoid attacks form one of the most universal and commonest symptoms in the group of diseases which we reckon among the mental diseases and neuropathies; the mere appearance of one or more epileptic or epileptoid attacks is not decisive for its course and prognosis. As mentioned, I have used the concept of epileptoid in the widest sense for the attack itself."[°]

The epileptoid moments of our case are not far to seek; the objection can, however, be raised that the colouring of the whole picture is hysterical in the extreme. Against this, however, it must be stated that every somnambulism is not *eo ipso* hysterical. Occasionally states occur in typical epilepsy which to experts seem parallel with somnambulic states,[†] or which can only be distinguished by the existence of genuine convulsions.[‡]

[°] C. Westphal, "Die Agoraphobie," *Arch. f. Psych.*
[†] Pick, *Arch. f. Psych.*, XV. p. 202.
[‡] *Allgem. Zeitschr. f. Psych.*, XXI. p. 78.

As Diehl shows,[*] in neurasthenic mental deficiency crises also occur which often confuse the diagnosis. A definite presentation-content can even create a stereotyped repetition in the individual crisis. Lately Mörchen has published a case of epileptoid neurasthenic twilight state.[†]

I am indebted to Professor Bleuler for the report of the following case: —

An educated gentleman of middle age — without epileptic antecedents — had exhausted himself by many years of over-strenuous mental work. Without other prodromal symptoms (such as depression, etc.) he attempted suicide during a holiday; in a peculiar twilight state he suddenly threw himself into the water from a bank, in sight of many persons. He was at once pulled out and retained but a fleeting remembrance of the occurrence.

Bearing these observations in mind, neurasthenia must be allowed to account for a considerable share in the attacks of our patient, Miss E. K. The headaches and the teno-

---

[*] "Neurasthenische Krisen," *Münch. Med. Wochenschr.*, März, 1902, "When the patients first describe their crises they generally give a picture that makes us think of epileptic depression. I have often been deceived in this way."
[†] Mörchen, *"Ueber Dämmerzustände,"* Marburg, 1901, Fall. 32, p. 75.

synovitis point to the existence of a relatively mild hysteria, generally latent, but becoming manifest under the influence of exhaustion. The genesis of this peculiar illness explains the relationship which has been described between epilepsy, hysteria and neurasthenia.

Summary — Miss Elise K. is a psychopathic defective with a tendency to hysteria. Under the influence of nervous exhaustion she suffers from attacks of epileptoid giddiness whose interpretation is uncertain at first sight. Under the influence of an unusually large dose of alcohol the attacks develop into definite somnambulism with hallucinations, which are limited in the same way as dreams to accidental external perceptions. When the nervous exhaustion is cured the hysterical manifestations disappear.

Emma and Carl Jung

Jabberwoke Pocket Occult Collection

CRYSTAL GAZING by Frater Achad

Thus, it is hoped, all will be satisfied; and should the satisfaction be equal to that of the Author at th opportunity to herald the Light – however faintly – the Ultimate Crystalline Sphere.

ISBN: 978-1-954873-36-0
$ 11.00 USD
FraterAchadCrystalGazing.com

HEAVENLY BRIDEGROOMS by Ida Craddock

"One of the most remarkable human documents eve produced... This book is of incalculable value to ever student of Occult matters. No Magick library is comple without it" – A.C.

ISBN: 978-1-954873-21-6
$ 14.00 USD
HeavenlyBridegrooms.com

MOONCHILD by Aleister Crowley

The cattiest & messiest novel from the transcriber of th Wickedest Man in England. Hiding behind the guise fiction, Moonchild is the Beast's platform to slander h many nemeses inside the spiritualist circles of London

ISBN: 978-1-954873-53-7
$ 19.00 USD /
AleisterCrowleyMoonchild.com

THE KYBALION by Three Initiates

There is no portion of the occult teachings which ha been so closely guarded as the fragments of the Herme Teachings, the Great Central Sun of Occultism, wh rays have illuminated the teachings promulgated since time.

ISBN: 978-1-954873-08-7
$ 14.00 USD
ThreeInitiatesKybalion.com

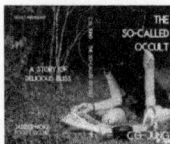

THE SO-CALLED OCCULT by Carl Jung

A 20-year-old Carl Jung attends his cousin's seanc leading to a psychological investigation of hauntin witch-sleeps, and delicious bliss that unravels i obsession.

ISBN: 978-1-954873-39-1
$ 14.00 USD
TheSoCalledOccult.com

THE GREAT GOD PAN *by Arthur Machen*

A classic of pagan horror that follows the trail of destruction left in the wake of a mysterious socialite, as she serves the will of her shadowy, horned benefactor.

ISBN: 978-1-954873-35-3
$14.00 USD
AllHailPan.com

THE WITCH CULT *by Margaret Murray*

Firsthand accounts of a pre-Christian witch cult that worshiped the Horned God of fertility—whose Christian persecutors referred to him as the Devil—and the nocturnal rites performed at the witches' Sabbath.

ISBN: 978-1-954873-33-9
$19.00 USD
TheWitchCult.com

THE BOOK OF LIES *by Frater Perdurabo*

A collection of falsehoods from Dionysus, received by the mysterious Frater Perdurabo and the Scarlet Woman LAYLAH. This wicked book is said to contain within its pages the secret truth of the universe . . . readers beware.

ISBN: 978-1-954873-37-7
$14.00 USD
FaleslyCalledBreaks.com

A MIDSOMMAR NIGHT'S DREAM *by William Shakespeare*

The timeless ethereal tale of four Lovers who wander too close to the games of Titania and Oberon, the Faerie Queen and King, and their encounters with the archetypal Tickster Puck and all the fantastical beings whom inhabit the woodland realm.

ISBN: 978-1-954873-54-4
$11.00 USD
MidsommarNightsDream.com

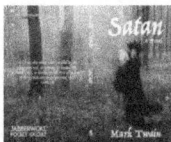

SATAN: A NOVEL *by Mark Twain*

The greatest and final novel from the master of American fiction, Mark Twain's fable of an angelic visitation in the Austrian countryside reveals the solipsism of its author, and his belief of the unreality of our collective dream.

ISBN: 978-1-954873-59-9
$16.00 USD
MarkTwainSatan.com

Wholesale Inquiries:
contact@jabberwokebooks.com

www.ingramcontent.com/pod-product-compliance
Lightning Source LLC
Chambersburg PA
CBHW022055020426
42335CB00012B/696